HOW YOU CAN HELP OTHER PEOPLE

BOOKS BY

SAMUEL M. SHOEMAKER

CONFIDENT FAITH
CALVARY CHURCH, YESTERDAY AND TODAY
CHRIST'S WORDS FROM THE CROSS
THE CHURCH CAN SAVE THE WORLD
CHILDREN OF THE SECOND BIRTH
CHRIST AND THIS CRISIS
THE CONVERSION OF THE CHURCH
GOD'S CONTROL
THE GOSPEL ACCORDING TO YOU
IF I BE LIFTED UP
NATIONAL AWAKENING
RELIGION THAT WORKS
TWICE-BORN MINISTERS

How You Can Help
Other People

By

SAMUEL M. SHOEMAKER

E. P. DUTTON & CO., INC.
NEW YORK

To

H. S. S.

*Dear Companion
in Life and Work*

CONTENTS

HOW YOU CAN HELP OTHER PEOPLE

I

The Need to Help People Today

IT IS HUMAN to like to help people. When an accident
happens on the street, people gather, not just from curiosity, but also to see if there is anything they can do; and
usually one or two of them are very useful. If a family is
made homeless by a fire, there are usually neighbours to
open their houses and tide the family over. When people
are sick, or in trouble, we go to see them or send them
flowers. There is an enormous flow of kindness between
the poor, sharing often in very sacrificial ways. We give
to the community chest, the Red Cross, the "neediest
families." We like to know something of the people to
whom we give, even through impersonal agencies. America
has its faults; but it is perhaps the most generous nation on
earth. It knows how to help, and it loves to help, in large,
material ways. It does not take saints to want to help
people: it only takes human beings.

But when we try to do more than meet the more super-
ficial needs of people (usually material), we often discover two things: first, the immediate need which is simple
often goes back to a deeper need that is more complicated;
and second, we feel inadequate to handle the intricacies
and complexities of a whole human situation. For instance, we give some money to a man who comes to the
door and asks for it: but if we try to do a thorough job,
we may run into a nature with difficult trends in it, or a
family problem, which cannot be handled by giving him

fifty cents or a dollar. This has led many of us into a policy of 'hands off,' and we delegate such responsibilities. Naturally we turn over a sick person to a doctor. Or a person needing legal advice to a lawyer. But then this process keeps on. For a maladjusted person, we call in a psychiatrist, or social worker. When a man cannot find employment, we suggest government relief. A very large number of people are thus made to become dependent on the government, with all the increased bureaucracy and impersonalness and politics which this may entail. And still more people are not dealt with at all—we beg the question of helping them, because it is simply too much for us.

Often we say to ourselves, "What can one individual do by working with other individuals in a day like this? Great collective schemes are in effect today, not only in the overthrown totalitarian countries, but in the democracies as well, which make what an individual can do seem like a drop in the bucket of human need." But, as we think of it, all this makes the need for helping individuals so much the greater. The distinctive liberties which have come to us through what is roughly called Christian civilization are in danger of being filched from us by such wholesale methods. Our safe way in the past has been for independent people to make their will known to the government, not for the government to decide what is good for them. We see the overshadowing of the individual contribution and initiative, and even worth, by huge social schemes which never work out quite so well in human life as they do in the paper plan. The sound particles of a sound society are happy, free, integrated, unselfish, positive people. The direct relation between these people are what hold families, communities, businesses, nations together. As Jacques Maritain says,[1] "Friendship is the true cause of civil peace. It is the animating form of society . . . So-

[1] *The Rights of Man and Natural Law*, p. 36.

ciety cannot exist without the perpetual gift and the perpetual surplus which derive from persons, without the
wellsprings of generosity hidden in the very depth of the
life and liberty of persons, and which love causes to flow
forth." With all the respect we may hold for proper legislation, for a fairer economic order (insofar as this can
be created except through just and fair relations between
people), it must be evident that things like "friendship,"
"gift," "surplus," "wellsprings of generosity" are only
found in people and are only expressed to other people.
They mean actual living relationships, knowing one
another, caring for one another, seeking to find richer life
for one another. Yet Maritain says these are the sources
of "civil peace," and that society cannot exist without
them. The old theory that there is a personal order, and a
social order, rigidly separated, is an exploded theory. The
two interact and impinge constantly upon each other. One
is no more important than the other, any more than one
leg is more important than the other if a man wants to
take a walk.

We are very much in the grip today of what Lord Elton
calls "the cult of the Plan." A 'Plan' spelled with a capital
P means something that has been worked out by somebody
else, by experts thinking in terms of masses of people, carried out by central government orders. These things may
be the first steps towards totalitarianism, the first surrender of faith in the democratic-Christian way of society.
We know that now. Certain national and social crises
seem to call for such centralized planning: but as soon as
the crisis is passed, we should begin to expect a greater
initiative from people themselves.

We are faced with the enormously critical immediate
post-war years. Some vast planning must be done. The
victory took vast planning. The policing of enemy and
formerly occupied countries took planning on a huge

scale. The supplies of food and clothing being sent into a score of countries, the medicine that must prevent further spread of disease,—these things could not be arranged by private initiative. Yet will these things alone be enough? It is not only men's cities that have been seared and pillaged; it is their souls also. It is not their funds only that are gone, but their faith. In place of the 'four horsemen' of War, Famine, Pestilence and Death, another ghastly quartette will be riding together: Fear, Hate, Revenge and Despair. You cannot tackle these things in quantity production: they arise in people, and must be met in people. Only other people can really touch and allay them. As we must provide for the material needs of exhausted men and nations on a colossal scale, we must seek to provide also for their inner and spiritual needs on no less a scale. This means training thousands, yes, millions of people in the art of getting on with other people, and of helping them.

There is no way to estimate the extent of the calamity of our time in its effect on people's basic beliefs about life. The full extent of what has taken place will be known, even to us in countries where news is relatively uncensored, only when the war has been over for some time. A traveller from Europe last year told me this story. A friend of his in Germany who had been able to keep in touch somewhat with the outside world, and to know what Germany was doing and how the other nations were reacting to it, made friends with another young German who was blindly loyal to the Nazi party. After they had become real friends and confidence was established between them, he took it upon himself one night, in a conversation of about four hours, to tell this young Nazi just what was taking place. And the young Nazi had a nervous breakdown. Said my friend from the other side, "I think Germany will be a nation with a nervous breakdown." Will it be confined to Germany? Now that the tensions of war are relaxed, and men are free to become themselves again, we shall find out how little of their old 'selves' remains. We in America are not exempt from this. We must remember that 24% of the men rejected for military service were refused, not on physical, but on psychological grounds. Four out of every ten men let out of the army for psychological reasons come from broken homes; which puts the root of the trouble back in civilian and parental laps. Thousands of men are coming back who will need, not only medical and psychological help, but a deep understanding on the part of all those with whom they come in contact. Never was it so important for the ordinary person to know how to help others as it is today.

For many years psychologists have been studying human personalities with a view to working out a science of the mind and spirit. Probably we have all benefitted from this effort, and most of us have taken into our minds more psychological ideas (some true, some false) than we realize. Obviously, there are limitations to any 'science' that attempts to be 'exact' when it comes to the enormously varied and complicated elements in human personality; not only do men differ much from each other, but we differ from ourselves at different times and under different circumstances. Above all, psychology is distinctly out of order when it ceases to be a method, and goes in for creating a philosophy: it is usually such psychology which has done harm. The method of psychology, and the fundamental values of human life, are very different things. Nevertheless, we can gain great understanding from psychology. It helps us to approach people empirically, deductively. It helps us to understand ourselves, and therefore to understand others.

There is another factor in helping people quite as important as knowledge; and that is faith. Insofar as doctors or psychologists effect real and lasting results, they do it by something more than the use of their knowledge of medical or psychological laws: they do it by their own encouragement and hope, by their own caring and faith. These may be the decisive factors; they are always important ones. I worked for years with one of New York's best-known psychologists, trying to help a man whose emotional apathy put him almost beyond the reach of any help at all. Along with his expert knowledge, the psychologist became real friends with this man, and showed him such personal kindness as made it evident that he was deeply anxious to *see him get well*. The doctor knew that I was working on the side of faith, letting the man talk out his anxieties whenever he felt so disposed. Together we pulled him out, and he is a well, useful citizen today. What did it? Psychiatric and neurological knowledge, human kindness and interest in him, an exposure to working religious faith, and the combined effort and faith on the part of both doctor and minister that he *could and would get well*. There is nothing in psychology, per se, that has any dynamics in it: information, yes, and valuable information: but to a spirit in utter darkness and despair, it is not bare knowledge that matters, it is the love and faith of others. There are depths of conscious need and unconscious need, of unrousable apathy, of almost impenetrable loneliness, of settled despair, which nothing can reach except the deep interest and faith of some other human being that one can be better. Indeed, we must never leave anyone to the ministrations of science alone, medical or psychological: in lesser needs, human sympathy is a help; in greater, it is indispensable. Faith changes the atmosphere of any situation. I have known a man die in a psychological institution, not from his sickness, but from sheer despair caused by his being allowed to have no contact whatever with people that had faith, and depended on it as he did. Love creates faith, and faith creates hope, and hope creates health. There is no way of computing the power of faith, nor its contagious effect.

The basis of this book is profoundly Christian. The writer believes that Christ was the greatest psychologist that ever lived, and intuitively and spiritually anticipated what we know of the mind today. A brilliant Scotch theologian, Dr. G. A. Johnston Ross, once said, "Psychology *crawls* to catch up to the Christian religion!" Not only in the clues He offers to the understanding of human nature and its problems, but in providing such standards and values and spiritual dynamics as will keep people from falling into many difficulties, and in giving them a focus round which to center the new way of living which they find when they discover the reality of faith, Christ has no competitor. The lives best trained from childhood in the art of living, the lives most able to adjust to Life as a whole, the lives best able to meet the problems that confront them in actual experience, the lives best grounded in an effectual and satisfying 'way of life' for the future, seem to be those which look to Him as their Guide.

I find no conflict, therefore, in approaching people empirically, with a view only to helping them with their needs; and in approaching them with the Christian faith in one's own heart, longing to communicate itself to them. To want to help a man in his present situation and out of a present need, and to want to help him find the dynamic of such a faith in life as Christ can impart to him, may be two sides of the same desire. They are as closely connected as disease and remedy. What use in finding out what is the matter with a sick man, if you have no cure to offer him? What use to analyze and take apart and then try to put together again the pieces of a man's inner life, if you can give him no new principle on which to go forward, no new dynamic by which to live and keep above his former needs? A highly intelligent business man asked me once, "when do you feel you have a right to ask another person to accept your belief?" And I said, "Only when that other person has begun to see that my faith may hold the answer to his problems."

Here is another important question: How far can a layman be expected to do this delicate and difficult work? It all depends upon how much he wants to do it, and will therefore give time and study, so that he may learn enough to make him effective. I have heard an eminent divine question the capacity of laymen for such work; but Dr. L. W. Grensted, professor and psychologist at Oxford University, once said in my hearing that he would rather trust a person in great need to a Christian undergraduate with a real reverence for human personality, than to a materialistic professional psychologist. In things psychological, I am myself a layman: I have learned just enough to know what I do not know, and when to call in a trained expert. Anybody can learn that much who has reasonable common sense. The need today is of such proportions that professionals cannot be had in sufficient numbers. The Rev. Russell S. Dicks, who has made a long study of the relation between medicine and faith in helping people, says, "Unless we can enlist the services of hundreds of persons, in addition to our professional workers, who will prepare themselves and give time to those who are going through these personal crises, the mental health and morale of our nation may suffer serious damage in the years ahead, particularly during the post-war years when the heat and excitement are passed and we enter our convalescent and rebuilding period."[2]

The clergy ought to be foremost in the ranks of those who do this work, and they ought to train their lay-people to do it. Yet how many clergy are "too busy" to

[2] *The Ministry of Listening,* Russell S. Dicks (Federal Council of Churches).

give more than a minor fraction of their time to helping people in need! Far too typical is a minister widely known, with a huge congregation and staff of workers, a magnificent church and equipment, who says, "I am driven day and night, often speaking out beyond where I have had a chance to think." Would anybody in trouble seek out this ecclesiastical edition of the 'tired business man' for spiritual help, for the replenishment of their used-up spiritual resources? No man can be convincing who hands out advice he is not following himself: the stuff withers on his lips. A humble and very honest bishop across the seas writes to me, "I think I'd love to be on your staff and have personal work to do instead of this long-range shooting." It is my belief that the clergy must revolt against much of the spiritually useless activity which clutters up their lives: endless speaking engagements, where at best little more is done than to make an impression of brilliance; committee meetings with little accomplished; and worried talks about the budget,—and get down to the meeting of those human needs which Christian faith alone can meet. I do not belittle the need for Christian institutions, and I do not underestimate the worth of good preaching: but I know that when these are not buttressed by personal dealing, they accomplish far less than we like to think they do. One clergyman friend of mine says frankly, "I do not love people." Another talks much about fellowship, but never admits anyone behind a certain invisible but very palpable barrier. A leader in American Protestantism sends a man on the verge of divorce to another clergyman with the brush-off, "He knows more about these things than I do." *Why* doesn't he know about them? Is he really afraid to be cooped up with a man, his problem— and God? Who is supposed to know about "these things" if not a Christian minister? And where may people be expected to turn if they go to the Church for bread, and get stones like that? It is—I say it without question—it is primarily the work of clergy to help people in their needs; and this is the primary work of the clergy. It is useless for them to urge their people to do such work unless they are ready to lead in doing it themselves.

What shall we do about our natural modesty over attempting to get behind the scenes in the lives of other people? There is a normal reticence, amounting sometimes to an aversion, which makes us hold back. If this means real respect and reverence for other people, then let us remember that it is precisely these attitudes which should make us want to help them if we possibly can. But if it is fear of risk, fear of being misunderstood, unwillingness to learn by doing (which requires some failure), then it is simply an inhibition which must be overcome. Let us not be too self-conscious and professional about it all, but remember that it takes a great deal of living before we shall have either the right or the opportunity to do very much talking. If we live by faith ourselves, if we let God help us in meeting the problems of life day by day, this will become evident to those whom we want to help. Unless they have a pressingly acute problem, we may have to wait during a time when we can only pray for them; but when the need arises, they will turn to the person who, by his life, and by his caring, has kept the door open.

We cannot estop our constant influence over people—every day there goes on the silent, unheralded impact of one person upon another—sometimes for good, sometimes for evil—it takes place in uncountable measure wherever human relationships exist. We are making life happier, stronger, finer, more worth-while by what we are and by what we do and by what we say—or we are making it sadder, weaker, meaner. It is not only the wicked people who drag the level down, but the drifters, the casual, the careless, the unthinking, the ineffectual.

The Need to Help People Today

The need today for strength to meet the problems of life is perhaps greater than it has ever been. In times of crisis we all give beyond what we ordinarily give: this is a time of great moral and emotional crisis for millions, and we must give in unprecedented ways. As healthy people in war-time give blood to save wounded bodies, so emotionally healthy people must give friendship and understanding to repair wounded minds. All of us who have been spared the harrowing tragedy of actual warfare, or come through it unhurt, all of us with healthy bodies and unimpaired minds, with normal emotions and sane outlooks, with faith and a relish for life left in us, have got something to give in the post-war years that is as urgently needed as blood for blood-banks in the time of war. We who have lived in comparative safety, and kept our health of body and mind, now have our innings of service: we are the favored, the privileged, the 'haves.' To us the distraught, the bewildered, the sad, the apathetic, the embittered, the vengeful, the weary, have a right to look for understanding, for strength, for help in getting back to emotional 'normal.' We must stir ourselves from our selfishness, and from slipshod and hit-or-miss methods of trying to help people in real need.

In face of this need, let us ask the Father of our spirits to give us wisdom and understanding and patience and skill, and to make us fellow-workers with Himself in helping all whom we can touch to find the fullness of life

II

What It Takes to Help People

WHAT ARE the qualities which must be developed in those who expect to help others?

If we want to help people we must *love* them.

Some of us say we love people, when what we mean is that we find a certain exhilaration in them, or that we are easily touched by distress. This is merely to say we belong to the human species. Mere natural love for people is an attractive quality in anybody, and may be a very useful factor in the kind of love we mean; but if it is just raw, instinctive and selfish, it may need to be refined and given much more direction. Real love for people must be unselfish; it must live on their territory and in their concerns. It must be able to take a large look at them, and to want greatly for them the fullness of life which God wants them to have. Real caring for people brings about a two-fold activity: it gives us a certain power to get 'inside' them, seeing life through their eyes, sympathy; and then it gives an energy which when added to their own makes the burdens lighter and the going easier. The fact that another person is intelligently interested in you and will take time and trouble for you brings a new factor into life and situations. Love is the most creative thing in the world.

But this love must not be sentimental. Sentimental love accepts the situation as the person himself describes it, and tries to find the remedy which he himself wants; and this may lead to all kinds of mistaken kindness. I know a rich woman who is beset by people who think that a gift of money will get them out of all their troubles: enough flattery and 'sob' talk, and they usually get what they want. The truth is that such giving is only a sop to both sides: it puts off the day when the receiver must face himself and get down to his real problems; and it wins for the giver a fawning gratitude which only inflates her ego. Sentimental love keeps people stuck in the problems from which we say we want to release them; it goes on trying to help people who have shown they are not in earnest about getting to the root of the problem; it steals the time which we might put into those who mean business; it puts great temptation in the way of those who want to be helped superficially. Let us give any amount of time to weak people who want to be strong, to people who are honestly trying to learn; but let us not waste time on those who come back again and again wanting us to mop up for mistakes they keep making because they will not get to the real root of the difficulty. Creative love has salt in it: it is very different from sentimental love.

We must keep in mind the difference between the will to love and the will to power. Love for people will keep drawing out of them the thing which their deepest natures want and crave, and this is usually not far from God's will for them. But the "will to power" is a will of one's own for them, which involves something to 'put over.' Thoreau once said, "If I knew for a certainty that a man was coming to my house with the conscious design of doing me good, I should run for my life."[1] We want everyone we seek to help, to find faith and abundant life and the greatest usefulness they can enjoy; but if we love them, we shall seek for at least the seeds of these things within them, whereas the desire to dominate them will be so full of one's

[1] "Economy" in *Walden.*

[23]

own ambition for them that it will tend to be unapprecia-
tive and so to lose their confidence. If we meet people with
ambition in our hearts towards them, even the determined
ambition that we shall help them, we shall find that it dries
up the springs of our sympathy and imagination, and we
shall work in the grip of a formula instead of by the inspiration of the Spirit. The will to love cannot stand side
by side with the will to power: they cancel each other out
like light and darkness. The pressure of one will against
another sets up resistance; whereas the realization that we
are actually talking with them only about that which they
really want, only asking them to do that which in their
heart of hearts they know they ought and want to do,—
this will make them know we have no cut-and-dried formula nor plan which we seek to fit on them like a harness.
Let us never begin to help someone conscious that we are
going to help them: let us begin by seeking to know them,
understand them, love them—and the help, if any there is,
will be as unconscious as it is inevitable.

If we are to help people, we must keep *emotionally detached* from them.

The work we are describing needs personalness and impersonalness—a warm interest and a cool detachment. We
must help people with their problems, but we must be
careful not to try to live their lives for them, nor to make
their decisions. We must help them out of an emotion of
disinterested love. We should let no more emotion come
into the situation than is brought by the normal joy of
helping people. We must avoid becoming involved with
people, so that they feel that they can lean on us very
much; or in such wise that we worry unduly about them.
If we are to keep healthy and objective about intimate
work with people, we should never take their problems to
bed with us and lie awake over them: say your prayers for
them, commit them to God; and then pull down a shade

in your mind which shuts out human problems, and you will be readier for the inspiration which may come to you early the next morning, and you will be refreshed with that physical energy which is most assuredly needed in living into the lives of people.

When we are able to help people, life-long friendships with them may result. But sometimes when we have done what we could, the ways will part. We must leave them free to retreat, only warning them if this means the refusal of a challenge we have put to them. In cases where they have become too dependent upon us, we may urge such a retreat. It should never be possible for them to hurt us by anything that they do, and if we experience 'hurt feelings' we may be sure too much personalness has crept in. If they resent our approach, it is time to withdraw or try another variety, but not a time to be resentful ourselves. If they take what we meant by kindness as an intrusion, the trouble may lie in the way we made the approach. If they do not take our advice, or welcome our help, that is their concern, not ours, except that we may learn where the approach could have been better. Our ability to keep emotionally detached, at the same time as we are deeply interested, is the true test of the quality of our help.

If we are to help people, we need a *knowledge of what life is*.

Some people get in difficulty, and many miss the mark, because they try to live in a world of their own making, not in the world that is. They often want help from people who assist in keeping up this illusion. Carried to extremes, wishful thinking can and sometimes does lead to split personalities and insanity. But in any degree it is dangerous. We shall help people most if we help them to understand what life is.

We must begin with a choice between what Dr. Richard Cabot called "pleasant fortune," and "spiritual training," as the end of life. Millions of people want its aim to be "pleasant fortune," and because such is not the case they are continually in a warfare with the constitution of things. If we accept "spiritual training" as the aim of life, we shall not expect it all to be smooth sailing: we shall only seek that, whatever happens to us, we may be drawn towards that supreme end.

The more we watch life, the more does it become plain that it is never *what happens to us* that is of supreme importance, but *how we take it*. A man is stricken with infantile paralysis: his hopes crash, he will not exercise painful muscles, he draws life about him like a curtain and becomes an invalid. Another man is hit with the same disease: he studies, he fights boredom with routine, he waits for the opportunity to come back into the world with the added knowledge and maturity of painful years, and makes a gallant life. The difference is not in the circumstance: the difference is in the way the man met the circumstance, that is, it is in the man himself.

Trouble comes to everybody, and almost indiscriminately. There is no relation between a man's virtue and his prosperity, nor between his rascality and his adversity. Disobedience to certain laws will bring on difficulty; but obedience in one area of life is no guarantee against misfortune in some other. Such trouble is not punitive, though it often has a warning value: it is part of the training of life itself; it is like the handicaps in a race. Religious faith is not a guarantee against trouble, but against defeat. A man is not to seek faith in God in order to ward off difficulty; if he does, he is doomed to disappointment. Faith does not alter what life brings to us, it alters what we bring to life, it alters the *way we take* what life brings to us. Pain, sorrow, loss, disappointment, death—no one can wholly escape these. But rebellion, self-pity, resentment, sulking, despair—everyone can escape these. The

{ 26 }

crucial thing in life is not what happens to us, but how we take it.

There is one quality which draws people, and opens the door to helping them, and that is *cheerfulness*. People are inclined to accept help from those they think to be making a good 'go' of life themselves; and if they have found the path, their cheerfulness ought to be the outward sign of it. A very thoughtful naval officer once told me that he thought the greatest factor in making children love their homes, and want to go back to them, is the factor of cheerfulness in their parents. If you look for the most obvious element in what laymen call a 'human' parson, it is likely to be his cheerfulness. No wonder Jesus often said to His friends, "Be of good cheer," which means precisely, "Cheer up!" The serious business to which they had put their hands tended to make them serious; maybe a frown or a solemn look came over their faces: and then He, Who was leading the most important work in the world, would say to them, "Cheer up!" Nothing is more unattractive and nothing is more obvious than fictitious cheerfulness. There are people who smile with their lips, but not with their eyes; or who put on a frozen religious smile. You can spot it at once, and most people want to run from it. But the person who is cheerful, not from self-satisfaction, and not because life is always easy, but because he knows "the way" and is finding his satisfaction in following it, is always a good drawing card for the faith he professes.

Of course the greatest need of all, if we would help people, is *faith*.

Faith is much less an intellectual matter than one of imagination. The mind can analyze; but the imagination can see things in a new conformation. Our own belief that things can be different or better for someone else goes back to what has taken place in our own lives; a letter on my desk says, "Mr. W's position is not easy and he has so much to put up with, but if God could handle the situation, what a difference, as we know who have tried it." That writer not only believes there is a God, but that God changes things when people live and act in faith. Such faith as this does not necessarily mean a vast accumulation of religious knowledge : it does mean a deep, true surrender of ourselves to as much as we know of God and His will. Faith is like a bicycle : it only stands upright when it is in motion—the minute it stops moving, it flops on its side. Faith means a great expectation, living right up into the very most a situation can yield, praying and working for that utmost. This is the faith that removes mountains, and makes men whole. People do not enter into it when they understand "all mysteries and all knowledge," but when they simply turn themselves and their needs over to God, go to work with Him, and let Him go to work with them.

We must learn to help people to cut in on the current of faith, and channel it to their needs. I was called to see a brilliant older woman whose husband had died, and who was utterly without any living faith. She was steeped in grief, in useless brooding and regret. We made friends. I talked with her about putting faith in place of despair. "How would you do this?" she asked. I said, "I'd simply get on my knees and ask God to lift that grief out, just as a man in a back-street mission asks God to take drink out." "Do you mean right here in my own drawing-room?" "What better place?" I asked. She was conventional, and it took courage ; but she did it—and from that day the seed of faith lodged and grew till Christ became the center of her life, and the joy He brought with Him was an astonishment to her friends as long as she lived.

Faith is like water, it can steal into the smallest openings. When you love someone, when you pray for him, and when God galvanizes your faith that things can be different for him, you have one of the most powerful forces on earth in your hands. Your faith lifts him for a time, not only to a new attitude, but to a new altitude, from which his life and problems seem different: then, if he catches the contagion of it, and begins living on faith himself, the new attitude and altitude become a permanent possession for him. Such faith is perhaps more often caught than taught; the fact that we have it, that it is a reality to us, will mean much more to another person than anything we say about it. Faith, its possession and transmission, is the heart of helping people.

But we need also *intelligence*.

The more we know of affairs, of the life of the world, the more points of contact we can establish with people and the easier it will be to gain their confidence and respect. But knowledge is less important here, perhaps, than good sense. There are many wise people who live wonderful lives yet are not much at home in the intellectual sphere. If we have knowledge of any kind, let us use it. If we can acquire it, we are neglectful and lazy if we do not do so. But the kind of horse sense that comes from observing life closely, and constantly bringing it under scrutiny from the standpoint of faith—anyone can acquire some of this.

We need to use our intelligence in the service of the person we want to help. That means concentration, attention. It means putting together the scattered scraps of self-revelation he gives to us consciously or unconsciously. Likes and dislikes, prejudices and personal demands, social habits, the flash of incipient anger in the eye, the unwillingness to get off the subject of self, even clothes and mannerisms—all these reveal something to a trained eye. We need to be "all there" when we are talking with people. Distrait and hurried attitudes may lose us the clue we need, or cause people to think we are not really interested. I suspect one reason why many people go to psychiatrists is that they are assured of the undivided, intelligent interest of a trained man for as much time as they are willing to pay for. The people who stand for faith must be prepared to give the same kind of intelligent and undivided help. Here is perhaps our largest opportunity to extend living faith, to seed it into the ground of society through re-made men and women. This will take all the intelligence we can command.

Intelligent dealing with people will cause us to be careful of our language. Worn-out religious language and overworked clichés are a positive hindrance. Professional jargon does two things: it baffles, and it nettles. Some doctors and psychiatrists are as bad as old-fashioned evangelists in this respect; they think the rest of us know what they mean by their heaped-up scientific words and phrases. A recent writer, blaming the use of complicated jargon in government publications, calls it "gobbledygook." Well, that's as good a word as any for saying things in a way ordinary people cannot understand. Intelligence means good adaptation. We would do well to follow the advice of Sam Jones, a famous character in the South of half a century ago, who once advised some theological students: "Don't put the hay so high the mules can't get at it. Spread it on the ground, and then the jackasses and the giraffes can both get it."

Another quality we need is *flexibility*.

The great danger of learning how to do something is to think it can only be done that way, or that it should always be done that way. There is danger in writing a book like this, that instead of its provoking experiment and effort in the reader, he may want to adopt its 'method.' Really there is no method of dealing with people. We must learn the laws of the spiritual life, as an artist must learn the laws of painting, and then let their effect on us be subconscious, indirect. If we are in the grip of a 'method,' we shall be more concerned to carry out the method than to help the person.

What It Takes to Help People

We must first find out *where the person is,* and begin there
—not where we think he ought to be. Sometimes a too direct challenge, or too much talk, causes him to fall silent,
and we realize we are losing him. Then let us draw him out
quickly on something that interests him, and be sure that
confidence has been re-established before getting back to
the uncomfortable territory. We must be in the grip of
nothing but God's Spirit and the man's own need, sitting
and riding loose between the two. We need many stops to
our organ, and must know when to change our tempo and
our volume. As St. Francis de Sales said, "Those who
govern souls must make themselves all things to all men.
In order to win all men, they must be gentle with some,
severe with others, a child with children, a hero with
heroes, a weakling with weaklings: in short, an infinite
discretion is required if one is to be fit to meet the needs
of all." [2]

We must speak also of *moral integrity.*

The greatest hypocrisy of our day is the divorce which
often exists between people's public and their private life.
When we meet people to help them, we meet them in two
ways (1) as a friendly human being, and (2) as an informal yet true representative of responsible society. Of-
ficially we must stand for the right things. Then we must
also stand for them in our own lives, so that there is no
divergence between what we urge on others and what we
demand of ourselves. This does not mean perfection before
we can set out to help other people; but it does mean integrity. There is good reason to suspect any psychological
advice that goes outside the accepted Christian commandments—good reason because playing fast and loose with
this accumulated wisdom of the past sets up further conflicts in the person who does it, and more harm than help
ensues. Dr. C. G. Jung says, "The physician is called upon

[2] *D. L. Moody,* by Gamaliel Bradford, p. 280.

to face that task which he wishes the patient to face . . .
these guiding principles in therapy confront the doctor
with important ethical duties which can be summed up in
the single rule: be the man through whom you wish to influence others. . . . The fact of being convinced, and not
the subject-matter of conviction—it is this which has always carried weight."[3]

Again, this work requires an endless amount of *patience*.

Sometimes I see a young person who has set out en-
thusiastically to help someone else, meet indifference, or
resistance, or fail to stir up any reaction at all—or one
who has made several such attempts—and they are ready
to throw up the sponge. One has to remind them that, as
Dr. Fosdick said, a man is like an island—sometimes you
have to row all around him before you find a place to land.
It is said that George Müller worked with a man for sixty-
two years before he could really help him. It is hard not
to grow petulant with those who do not respond, especially
if we know they are in some kind of need: but there is no
substitute for the kind of patient waiting of a creative sort
that is like a fisherman sitting very quietly while he tries
many kinds of flies.

Sometimes also patience is needed to work through our
own bafflement. We try something, and it seems to be working—then suddenly everything comes to an end. Or we
just see no way that really offers a solution—nothing but
choosing the lesser of two evils. Our pride is often involved
in all this: we think we *ought* to know some way, and
therefore are tempted to act quickly and impetuously;
when what the facts call for is creative waiting till other
factors have emerged. It is legitimate to talk over even a
confidential human problem of a baffling kind with others
who know how to do this kind of work, provided we take
every precaution to guard the identity of the person we are

[3] *Modern Man in Search of a Soul*, p. 59.

talking about; sometimes this is the only thing that relieves our bewilderment. In time we shall learn that God *always* has His plan, but sometimes that plan includes our own patience.

But patience is not inconsistent with *persistence.* If God puts somebody on your heart, and they keep coming into your mind as you pray, He probably wants to do something for them through you. Can you keep a person, as it were, in the wings of your mind for a long time, mindful of them, praying for them, yet knowing that now is not the time to seek them out? Can you stand some indifference, some derision, some real persecution, for you may get some of each? Persistent friendliness with a little fillip of challenge now and then to show we are not unmindful of them, and then a smile or a wink to let them know we are not provoked at them—this may have to go on for a long time. It takes some courage to remain persistent. But think how persistent God has had to be with some of us . . . !

And let us never forget the need for *humility*—genuine, inner humility.

Lots of people think that humility is a kind of self-effacement which means doing nothing at all. Real humility, as I see it, is just one thing: it is depending on God, not on ourselves. It isn't inferiority, nor shyness, nor running away, nor everlastingly calling attention to how useless one is (this is really just pride back-firing): humility is depending on God. In this case, it is knowing that it is God who helps people, not we. This does two things: it keeps us from worrying about people when things are going badly; and it keeps us from pride when they are going well. Our work is to do what God tells us. If we fail, let us bring the failure to Him and ask for another chance. If we succeed, let us bring the success to Him, for it is His success, not ours. *'Non nobis, non nobis . . .'*

It is a tremendous thing to realize that we may be the

bridges between God and people. We often wish He would work in them directly, and sometimes He does. But sometimes also He wants an agent, an intermediary, a bridge. We know that we are not good enough for such work; as George Whitefield said, "My corruptions are so strong and my employment so dangerous that I am sometimes afraid."[4] We all feel this at times, if we have even a decent amount of humility. And then what temptation comes to us if we develop a lust to be known as a great spiritual influence! Power of any kind is scarcely to be borne by any human being; I have seen it go to the heads of men I thought surely immune to it. We need to watch it like the plague.

The inner cure to pride is thanksgiving: the more you are thankful to God, the less will you be thankful to yourself. But it wants an outer check also. And that comes from persuading the people about us not to take us for granted, and not to spare us from knowing how they feel. There are so few people among those who call themselves Christians that ever have about them a salty fellowship, willing to deal honestly with their faults. The average minister, for instance, usually gets no corrective, unless it be from his wife, until things have developed in a wrong direction so far that corrective is too late. Then his board of laymen, or his bishop, or events, correct him: but how much better if his wife, or one of his laymen, or someone on his staff, had told him frankly that his inattention to detail, his temper, his want of preparation of his sermons, his general disorganization, or his talkativeness, were spoiling his life and his ministry! We need to say to someone, perhaps to several, and to mean it so much that they know we mean it, what Fenelon said, "I ask of you with more earnestness than ever, that you will not spare me with regard to my faults. If your opinion of my defect

4 *D. L. Moody,* Gamaliel Bradford, p. 133.

gives me pain, this sensibility will prove that you have touched me in a tender part."[5] It is said that the Pope himself has his own confessor, and once a year is preached to in a several days' mission by a monk from one of the Orders. Human pride is the deadliest of the "seven deadly sins"; and the honest spoken word of a true friend is God's word—and if we will not heed it, may be God's judgment—to us.

Now let me suggest certain principles of helping people:

1. Let us begin always with a will to understand, not a will to criticize. If we put ourselves in the other person's position, we shall know how he came to do what he did, or to be what he is. The first thing that ought to strike anyone whom we want to help is *sympathy,* understanding. He will have been through some things which will surprise us, he may have done some things which will shock us. If we are right inside ourselves, we shall always be shocked by real human evil: but if we are right inside, we shall also remember our own sins, and we shall never let the person before us feel the sense that we are shocked—for if we do, we shall stop him from talking in perfect candour. Sometimes counsellors with strong religious faith and convictions break in with disapproval or censure so that the real facts never come out, and so the saving effect of a complete *catharsis* is not achieved. We do well to remember that in Christ God identified Himself with us men while we were yet in our sins—not with our sins, but with us in spite of our sins. We must always seek to do the same thing. We need to be perfectly clear on our moral principles, and never to compromise with them for one instant: but one can stand up for his principles with a smile that is gracious, or with a frown that speaks in the thunder of the Ten Commandments. We do not condone because we do not immediately condemn: it is not our function to do either, but to talk

[5] *Selections from Fenelon,* Follen, p. 241.

this man out of himself, and help him to understand himself, and help him to find a faith by which his whole life can be strengthened.

2. Let us listen more than we talk. What people say to us is often more important than what we say to them. Most religious people and those who represent the standards of the community, face to face with those in some kind of need or without faith, tend to talk too much. Especially do clergy do this; I have some notes taken when a parson was lecturing about the need to listen to men: but when you went to him, you always got a cross-section of a book he was writing, or a magazine article he was reading, so that you hardly ever got a word in edge-wise—and I knew one young man in his congregation in desperate need who went elsewhere *to be listened to*. Returning service men will need a chance to talk. The more they will talk with us, the more times they go over what happened, if they are held by obsessive thoughts of it, or have psychoneurotic reactions to it, the sooner will these thoughts wear off. A good, thorough, unhurried talk is like a good pelting rain on a street—it carries away the dirt and the more of it there is, the better the job is done. Sometimes people lose themselves in detail, and need a question or statement here and there to bring them back on the track, but not long preachments of our own pet theories. We are not talking something *into* them, we are talking it *out* of them. Let us keep among the great, undisputed realities, especially if we touch upon religion, and not draw their minds off on side issues. Let us keep quietly concentrated on the man's own need, not upon what his words may suggest to us, and not too much upon what answers we are going to give him. After all, it is not we who help people. Really they help themselves as they see themselves, and God helps them as they come into a greater dependence on Him.

3. Let us tell them, from our own or others' experience,

of things that have been helpful to us in solving our problems. Let us get as near to a situation like theirs as we can, and keep to experience, not theory. Nearly all of us have had actual help from God in time of trouble, or from another human being, or from an idea or a book. We need to get people up off the floor of floundering and self-dependence, to the upper storeys of working faith. We need not be preachy or censorious, but we can suggest better ways to handle a situation than they are taking. We can carry the cause back of the symptom to the root. I worked for hours over a returned service man, full of nerves: then I had to tell him one day that the real source of his unhappiness and confusion was a deep self-centeredness—he had not learned to live in God and in other people. I had been sympathetic and earned the right to go further and say the truth that was unwelcome but that healed. It is the truth that makes us free. So few people ever hear it: for we all see the truth about one another pretty clearly, tell it to others behind their backs, and then say to their faces what we think they want to hear. This is not friendship, it is not truthfulness, it is not helping people. The truth spoken in love is often God's best way to help people to see and understand themselves. Often, in fact usually, we can say this obliquely as a discovery we have made in our own lives; and the other person will take it up and make the application. Far better if it works out this way. But if it does not, let us not fear to suggest the application ourselves.

4. Let us spend real time in prayer for those we want to help. Prayer may be all that we can do for those who are not yet open, in whose life we have as yet found no place to land: it draws us closer to them as anyone will find who tries it; barriers of self-consciousness and resistance will sometimes melt away through the power of it. Prayer also brings insight. Sometimes while I am talking with people, listening to them with the forefront of my mind, and pray-

ing for them with the back of it, a thought will come into it that flood-lights the whole situation by showing me the root of the trouble. And when I say, "Do you think the real trouble may lie here?" there is sometimes a smile of agreement that shows we are on the way to a solution. If we have been praying *for* people, it may be natural also to pray *with* them. After all, if we are in league with a Great Power, and they begin to long for that same power, let us lead them right into His Presence. We all need prayer to keep ourselves out of the way, to let God into the situation.

5. We must provide fellowship for people whom we help. Nobody can get on with the New Life by themselves. One of the most useful things we can do for people under tension is to include them in our homes, letting them have part in real family life, not treating them too 'specially' but building back social confidence in them. Let us watch to see if they take to one member of the family, and would like to get where they can talk things out more fully. There ought to be in churches and communities groups where such people are included, made to feel at home, and to feel useful. A doctor who is working much with returned service men says, "The only way we can meet these problems is to understand the people who have them. And the only way we can understand them is to have the infinite patience to listen to them. In the sense that people are incurably in need of fellowship, they are incurably religious. And if the fellowship of the kind they need is not available with friends, in churches, and in other wholesome ways, they will get it in saloons, low-grade clubs, or subversive political movements. To do the job, people must care enough about these men to bother about them. It isn't the exact kind of activity that matters (dances and bingo games will not turn the trick) ; it is the attitude to the men. If there is spirit, warmth, real kindness, listening because one is

interested, acceptance of the man as he is—then the job will be done."[6]

None of us knows enough about helping people. But we shall not learn more about it until we begin to do it. A need faces us today perhaps greater than any that we have ever known. It should enlist the sympathy and interest and active coöperation of all who believe that the mind and the spirit of man are at least as important as his body, and who know that mental and emotional and spiritual wounds are in constant danger of being overlooked because their therapy depends upon a wise blending of the very new science of psychology and the very old faith of religion. One does not counsel amateur experimentation in so important a field; but one does ask for those who will learn all they can from others, and then learn more from experience and from working with God, till they become at least better trained and more skillful in the all-important work of helping people.

[6] Dr. Florence Powdermaker, in *The Church and Returning Service Personnel*—Federal Council of Churches of Christ in America.

III

Responsibility

IT IS GENERALLY true that we can only help people when they feel some sense of need and when they want to be helped. We may, however, cause them to become aware of a need they did not realize before by showing to them a kind of faith and zest in life to which they have hitherto been strangers, so that they begin to feel a need which is a kind of healthy envy. If you see a person with obviously radiant faith, you envy him—you can't help it. This awakens in you a sense of need that may not have consciously been there before. Part of our work, as we shall see later, is to arouse people's imaginations, to hold before them possible pictures of themselves that go far beyond their attainments or even expectations, but not beyond their desires. Nevertheless, until a sense of need exists, it is probable that we can do little to help them.

A sense of need is the troubled thought that things should and might be different and better than they are. We feel beaten or afraid, we feel drab and useless, we feel we are missing life's best. The easiest and perhaps the commonest thing to do is to lay the blame for the situation upon circumstances or someone else. We live a cramped, stultified little life—it is because circumstances flung us into a small town and we can never get out. We burn with a long-time rage against somebody; it may have been there so long that we have buried it almost out of consciousness—but it is the injustice of another that made the rage,—the brother who got away with most of the family money, or the person that persistently misunderstood us. There are trends in our nature that we charge up to an unfortunate heredity, or the wrong influences when we were children. It is comfortable to believe that most of our trouble and unhappiness is attributable to other people; and it is probable that this is the underlying cause of much personal conflict, of most divorces, of much that is unresolved between labor and management, and ultimately of war itself.

But the really mature viewpoint will reveal our own part in the difficulty which comes to us. Perhaps we have been objectively wronged by someone—most of us have. Was there anything in ourselves that caused them to act as they did? Is there a lesson to be learned from it? And whatever they did, they cannot affect our own response and reaction to what they did—that is our own. Nothing from without can really hurt us unless we let it. Remember it is not "pleasant fortune" we are here to seek and find, but "spiritual training." The really hopeful, and the really practical, place to look for the trouble and the answer is in ourselves, in our own reactions. We cannot control outside events. The wills and deeds of other men are in their control, not ours. But we can control the way we react to what others do, or to the seeming heartlessness of events themselves.

The refusal to consider our fundamental responsibility for our own lives and the lives about us (extending right on out to the whole world), the rejection of opportunity or the failure to meet it with all our powers, the choice of the lesser, cheaper way, is what Christianity has always called sin. We know today that sin is a vastly bigger thing than people thought who made it to consist in drinking, card-playing, theatre-going and adultery: we know that it is injustice, and intolerance, and inferiority, and the refusal to face ourselves, and spiritual ineffectualness. But the ex-

tension of the meaning of 'sin' to include wrong social attitudes as well as personal defeats always runs the risk of
knocking the point off it, so that we do not feel nor accept
our responsibility, so that we do not burn with shame and
disappointment at ourselves. Psychology has not always
helped us here: it often offers us long, excusing, explanatory words for what we know in our heart of hearts is our
failure to grip fully our responsibility, i.e. *sin*. We do not
like to turn away from blaming circumstances or other
people, and fix some of the blame on ourselves; but it is by
all odds the most honest, the most practical and the most
liberating thing that we can do. If the root of all the trouble
lies where we can't touch it, we are in a desperate case. If
even a portion of it lies at our own front door, then we can
do something about it—we can face it, we can make repa-
ration for it, we can seek release and forgiveness. To admit
our sins is positively the most cheerful thing any of us can
do. I never tire of quoting G. K. Chesterton on this: "The
glad good news brought by the Gospel was the good news
of original sin."[1]

It is now possible to talk about 'sin' without seeming
to be hopelessly divorced from all that the modern science
of the mind has discovered, as has for long been the case.
Hear these words of Dr. Karl Menninger,[2] "When the
theological doctrine prevailed that pain, disease and death
are related to sin (the wages of sin is death), it is logical
to direct prophylactic measures against sinfulness. For
some centuries medical science scoffed at this theory, and
related pain, disease, and death to external invasions of the
body and to idiopathic physiochemical alterations. But
today, after a long digression, we have in a measure come
back to the sinfulness theory. For, in repudiating this
theological tenet, modern science had reverted to the phi-

[1] St. Francis of Assisi by G. K. Chesterton, p. 39.
[2] *Love Against Hate*, p. 199.

losophy that man is the hapless prey, the potential victim of solely external forces, which is the philosophy of primitive man as well as of the helpless child; whereas to conceive of disease as related to sin recognizes the partial responsibility of the individual for his own fate."

It will explain a lot, and it will bring a lot of new hope into a situation, if people will admit the reality of sin, and face their own share of it. It is actually the first step in the new life; and most people will never find nor take that first step until they are honest with themselves about sin. Sin, in relation to man, is selfishness: sin, in relation to God, is the want of love for Him and therefore disobedience. The pride that wants to work out one's own destiny irrespective of God is the deepest kind of sin; perhaps next comes the refusal to go and say you're sorry when you have hurt somebody. To call sin by its real name is the first step away from it. A young woman spoke powerfully along this line at a meeting, and next day came a letter from a friend of hers who heard her, saying "You know, T——, I never felt like a sinner before—always I felt futile or frustrated or enraged, but not *personally* responsible for evil things. Now for the first time I do—but I'm not exactly downcast about it, either. I think a lot of my apparent defeatism has been an attempt to atone for my own sins actually . . . and we can't, and besides we don't need to, as Christ did that." In a few words, she has caught the whole Christian belief about sin: the reality of it, the hopefulness of facing it, the wrong way to deal with it and resultant failure, and the Cross as the real answer.

We shall not understand human nature, nor find an adequate remedy for its needs, unless we recognize the reality and the enormity of sin. Since Adam defied and disobeyed God, sin has been rebellion and mutiny in God's universe. And since Adam, there has been a connection between man's sin and his misery. The world lost its be-

lief in the reality of radical evil in this world, beginning
about the turn of this century: and this outlook makes the
best soil for radical evil to grow in, with the result that
we have seen a war of such horror and devastation as we
could hardly have conceived. Says Dr. D. Elton Trueblood,
"There is no known way to keep justice, mercy and truth
apart from a religious experience which moves men
deeply." Radical evil does not just exist, like moss that
feeds on air: radical evil is in the human will. Satan and
the human will—these are the sources of radical evil. Do
you dispute the desperate wickedness of the human heart?
I wish you had listened with me to a young son of privilege
who was divorcing a wife whom he had first enticed into
living with him, then married, who had borne him children,
and been a good mother to them. He was taking the action
on two grounds: first, that she would not join his church
which he thought was *the* church, and second (save the
mark) because she had been an immoral woman—yet he
had made her immoral! I could tell you plenty more like
that: sometimes after an interview it seems to me the walls
of my study reek till you could scrape the filth off them,
till it needs to be fumigated. It is not the sins of passion—
hate or the flesh—that leave behind them that kind of impression: it is the sins of the spirit—complacency, cruelty,
ingratitude, treachery. Do not be surprised as you travel
with a man through the rooms of his life to come upon one
closet which, when he unlocks it, belches forth the stench
of a skeleton, maybe several of them. Take no one senti-
mentally for granted. We need to be very alert, and to be
sure we have gotten to the bottom, and are not dealing with
symptoms.

The greatest weakness of the church today is its unreadiness to deal effectively with people's real needs. We
do not like to put these things up to people. As Reinhold
Niebuhr says, "I think the real clue to the tameness of a

preacher is the difficulty one finds in telling unpleasant truths to people whom one has learned to love."[3] Well, that is sheer funk. Medical doctors cannot so easily escape; it would be criminal not to deal with what they find, and some day the patient has got to know. But the clergyman is too delicately constituted, too gentle, too shocked by ruffled feelings,—no, let us say it honestly—too weak, too soft, too poor a shepherd and too little a man, to say the cutting, healing thing that, being the truth, can bring genuine cure and relief!

We must learn how to help people to call things by their right name, yet we must ourselves be without personal animosity or accusation. We must keep coming back again and again to the real trouble, till they admit and recognize it. It is very hard to keep one's patience while the man before you seeks every cover where he may hide his guilt, every excuse by which he may defend it, every delay to keep him from looking squarely at it. But the loss of temper or patience on our part is a sin. We lose ground by it. The work God is seeking to do is hindered by it. As Fenelon said, that great understander of the human heart, "When we blame with impatience because we are displeased with the fault, it is a human censure, and not the disapprobation of God. It is a sensitive self-love that cannot forgive the self-love of others. The more self-love we have, the more severe our censures."[4]

In the presence of a challenge to take another step forward that will cost something, there often develops what is called a *conviction of sin*. It is a very uncomfortable state of mind, and sometimes makes people do strange things. If one lets the conviction be the work and channel of the spirit of God, he will move on from it to repentance and real change of heart and life: that is its intended meaning.

[3] *Leaves from the Notebook of a Tamed Cynic*, p. 53.
[4] *Selections from Fenelon*, Follen, p. 243.

It is like the physical pain that indicates the need for medicine or an operation.

But if he refuses to take the next step indicated, conviction of sin works quite another way. Sin does not let go of life any more easily than we do: it fights for every inch of territory it possesses. The fundamental self-will in us all is roused to bitter opposition. This comes out in the following ways:

a. We lie about the real condition. Not only do we answer untruthfully a direct question: we carefully manipulate the situation so as to throw off the track even those with spiritual insight, and to cover up what goes on inside. In a meeting a group of professional men were becoming honest about themselves for the first time, after a quantity of general objective talk: they were frank about their failures, their sins, their need of God's grace. One of them, instead of welcoming this new candour, said he thought it unhealthy "subjectivism," he was never so happy in his work as today, and he gave off the impression that the others were back in the ABCs of life, while he was a graduate student. This particular man (I chanced to know) used to be in a good deal of psychological turmoil: either he had found a real answer which he ought to be glad to make available to others, or else he was covering up with a mask the real condition. Which do you think it was? Two other men left the room after speeches characterized rather by heat than light, one of whom had previously made a speech about those who leave meetings before they are over! To me it was a clear case of conviction of sin in the presence of a degree of reality which they were unwilling to accept.

b. We change the subject. That is what the Woman at the Well did, when Christ got uncomfortably close to the real moral need in her life. "Sir," she said, "I perceive that thou art a prophet. Our fathers worshipped in this mountain; and ye say, that in Jerusalem is the place where men ought to worship." That's called in slang a "red herring." That is trying to turn the conversation away from adultery to ecclesiastical technicalities. We have seen people do it dozens of time. Children do it naturally: we talk to them about picking up their room, or finishing their lessons; and they will suddenly become very interested in the price or origin of our neck-tie, or where we are going to take a vacation this summer. Any port in a storm—any other subject is good enough to get away from something we don't want to face.

c. We may be so miserable that we threaten or even commit suicide. The classic instance is Judas: the way back was as clear for him as it was for Peter. But pride would not let him take it, and a kind of stubborn despair was the confederate of pride. There is no misery under heaven like a deep conviction of sin which we will not let move on into repentance and freedom. I once saw a man enraged at his family, unwilling to face himself and make restitution, take his pistol and threaten to kill himself: he did not do it, others got the gun away from him, and I think he did not struggle much to prevent them; for all this was much more the show of self-pity, the dramatic gesture of the "misunderstood" than the real intention of a suicide. Threat of suicide is sometimes the back door for those who are convinced of sin and will not take the front door of repentance. In this kind of case, it is more a threat than a likelihood. It is actually the coward's way of getting quick attention; and needs a mixture of sympathy and straight dealing.[5]

d. We fight back. This may take the form of an attack on the personal character of the person who represents the challenge to us; we say he is tactless, or bad-mannered, or something worse. The *"argumentum ad hominem"* is not

[5] Where any serious mental factor is present in a case of threatened suicide, however, the help of a doctor should be sought.

a philosophical conception: it is often the weapon of many who wish to evade the challenge incarnate in somebody else. We pick flaws in what he says or does, and how he does it. We decry his associates or former actions. We personally dislike and oppose him. We keep out of his way, and harm his work and future. Every vital spiritual personality and movement, from St. Paul to Stanley Jones, has had its detractors and persecutors; mostly in the ranks of the convicted. Very little of the persecution of spiritual movements arises from a single-minded and disinterested concern for the welfare of religion: a great deal of it comes from a stung conscience. Let us be prepared for this. A religion of "vested interests" is almost the natural persecutor of a religion of the Spirit; and it does not always take very long for a religion of the Spirit to become a religion of its own "vested interests," whose means become ends, and which in turn persecutes the religion of the Spirit.

I have spent some time on this negative aspect of conviction of sin. It is scarcely understood by the Church and its workers today. In one seminary, a woman student under real conviction was thought by the faculty to be sick—so little touch had they had with the birth-pangs that precede spiritual deliverance! We must understand this kind of conviction; and know how many lukewarm opinions, and false judgments, how many wrong decisions, go back, not to want of facts or the power to judge them; but to a spirit that is crooked and awry through unfaced conviction of sin, fighting against the admission of any factor which keeps the conviction alive. Many souls are never born again at all because there was no one to go through these pains with them. It takes a terrible lot to kill the self out of us!

But there may be a hopeful outcome of such bitter conviction. I shall always remember a wise word I heard Professor Grensted, of Oxford, say: "Don't be disturbed at persecution. Remember that the opposite of love is not hate, but indifference. When you've got a man's hate, you've got his attention."

Conviction of sin means a consciousness of wrong within. When we have sinned, and when we have refused to call sin what we know in our hearts is sin, we feel a sense of guilt. Before God, when we have broken His laws, we are guilty. This makes sin sin, and not just misfortune or ill-fate. We might not have sinned, we could have taken a higher course instead of a lower: we are free and we used our freedom wrongly. This is sin, and it leads to a sense of guilt.

But there are some very important things which we must say about guilt. The first is that the object of the Christian religion is not to create a sense of guilt in us, but rather repentance and the acceptance of forgiveness. No wonder Dr. John MacMurray writes in *Creative Society*,[6] "The doctrine of forgiveness of sin has been almost more completely parodied by pseudo-Christianity than any other. A great deal of Christianity has actually so perverted the plain teaching of Jesus as to conceive that its first duty was to arouse and deepen in men, by all the means in its power, the sense of guilt. This is, of course, one of the subtlest means of destroying the spontaneity of any individual and making him amenable to the control of others. The whole problem of religion, as Jesus clearly saw, was to reverse this process; and so to create the kind of men who could not be imposed upon by authority through their own sense of guilt, but would spontaneously create from a sense of equality and freedom." We have seen precisely this happen again and again. It happens where the heavy weight of an ecclesiastical tradition keeps the individual in constant subjection to the system. It also happens where the cohesion of a religious movement is maintained by subjecting its indi-

[6] Quoted J. G. McKenzie, *Psychology, Psychotherapy and Evangelism*, p. 125.

vidual adherents to the will of the leaders or the company as
a whole. In both cases the sense of guilt is worked up, and
worked upon, to deeper a dependent loyalty in the believers.
Spontaneity means freedom: therefore spontaneity is
crushed out, and a continuous sense of guilt substituted for
it. The inducement of guilt for purposes of control is the
acme of spiritual malpractice: it is as bad for those who
impose and use it, as it is for those upon whom it is imposed. For master and slave, as Berdyaev has pointed out,
are neither of them free people.

After the problem has come to light, and the person has
been honest about his real self, we want to bring him the
reality of Christian forgiveness. In so many people, even
in those who have experienced a partial spiritual release,
there is the terrible back-drag of the past—a past they cannot shake off, cannot forget, but which continually discourages them. Nothing will ring down the curtain on the
past for good and all except forgiveness. Here psychology,
as we have already seen, cannot help us. I quote Dr. Grensted of Oxford again, "Psychology, for all its outward appearance of charity, knows no forgiveness, and is therefore harder and less true to reality than the sternest Cal-
vinism. For science is a matter of law and not of mercy,
and the doctor who is not something more than a scientist
has nothing to say to sin." Let us say to people something
of our own convictions about forgiveness, of what the
Lord's Prayer says and teaches about it, associating it always with the willingness to forgive those who have
wronged us. There is deep within many people who have
even the slightest knowledge of the Christian religion a
feeling about the Cross, that somehow the Cross does represent to men the love and forgiveness of God. How many
times have I knelt down in my study with some anxious,
burdened, defeated, bewildered person, who needed all the
relief of talking things out in leisurely and friendly fashion,

but whose deeper needs would have been missed entirely if we had not dropped on our knees, looked up at the Crucifix on the wall, and said our prayers, not to that piece of wood, but to the living Lord who hung on the Cross for us—and what fresh accessions of courage, faith, hope, new life have I seen stream in where forgiveness was consciously sought, with true penitence as the price, and truly accepted!

There is another important thing to be said about guilt. One finds today so much mental or physical sickness that is mixed up with sin, so much that is pathological and morbid in the way people sometimes think about their sins, that we must be very careful how we seek to increase the sense of guilt. The 'bad conscience' which is found full-bloom in the neurotic is found wide-spread today among those perhaps not quite to be classed as neurotic, but who yet are anxious, disturbed people; and this is not to be confused with a healthy conviction of sin in normal people. The nearer people are to being neurotic, the more important is it for us to remember that deliverance from their sins and the shame of them must be done in two steps. We must first help them towards getting emotionally well; and when they have begun to get well, then we can talk about the sense of sin. Those confused or in conflict in their inner life, and partly sick from it, cannot make a cleancut break with the past. It has taken them months or years to wind themselves up into this tension, it may take months or years for them to unwind; not to *begin* to unwind, but to unwind altogether. Our faith can be so contagious that they reach for it while they talk with us, and in so doing see that the past can be left behind, and maybe take a small step away from it. But they cannot face an objective condition of sin, and either feel the appropriate amount of guilt for it, or take the appropriate steps away from it, until they are less sick in mind. Therefore I do not think that the place to begin with such people is by talking too

much about guilt, or trying to superinduce it : they have too
much of it already, and it is of the wrong kind. As they
begin to get stronger inside, and come into possession of
their inner faculties, they can look sin square in the face,
and deal with it as at some time it must be dealt with. But
I think that, the sicker a person is in mind or emotions,
the more is the facing of guilt an *advanced spiritual step*,
not an elementary one. It is a step that should be faced some
way down the road, not where the road starts.

Our first contribution to those mentally or emotionally
sick (and thousands are on the verge of such sickness who
need to be held back from it) is to rescue them from mor-
bidity and defeat by the kindly grace of God. In many of
these people both the loss of faith and the presence of some
kind of defeat in their lives consequent upon the loss of
faith have created the present situation. Wrong-doing is
not only morally disruptive : it is emotionally and physically
deteriorating. People in this borderland between health
and sickness, between moral health and sin, need to be surrounded with the atmosphere, not of guilt, but of faith.
They need to be helped to take, not the great step of facing
the full reality of one's sin and guilt before the Cross of
Christ and accepting His full redemption, but the simple,
possible, available step of laying hold of a little bit of His
Grace through the faith of another person, by simple
prayer, by something quite elementary and recognizeable
that God does for them right then and there. This will
wear off, and need to be repeated—so does a bath—but
each time it is repeated it grows stronger. What has impressed me has been, not so much the difficulty and complexity of helping people under something more than the
usual emotional strain so that they have given away a little
under it, but the amazing amount of return that comes from
a very little spiritual investment in them, how almost un-
failingly they respond, and how soon they begin to be

better. We must look for some ups-and-downs; but these grow less frequent and less serious if we constantly meet such people on a basis of love, faith and prayer. Until such time as these people can take full responsibility themselves, we must, not exactly take it for them, but carry it with them. Growth comes for them, as for us all, by facing the next responsibility and meeting it to the best of their ability.

It is the Christian belief, and this is fortified by all we know of the human spirit, that men must face their responsibility for their lives, and yet need assistance if they are to do it effectively. When a high standard of conduct confronts human nature with a challenge, a tension is set up. The gap between the two constitutes the challenge. Just here comes in the essential psychological need of God. For when, without God, a man sets off to reach that ideal, insofar as he is successful it makes him proud, which negates the ideal; and insofar as he fails, it makes him discouraged and perhaps despairing of himself. But when, with God, he sets off to reach the ideal, insofar as he is successful it makes him thankful, which negates possible pride; and insofar as he fails, he seeks forgiveness, deeper dependence on God, and the courage of a fresh start. In other words, where we try, we need strength from outside ourselves. Where we fail, we need forgiveness. And where we succeed, we need Somebody to thank, else our success will go to our heads and produce pride. Here lies the deep psychological health of the Christian religion: it enables us to meet and progressively resolve the tension which it creates in us, due to the difference between what we are and what God wants us to be. We cannot bridge that gulf ourselves. The whole Christian Religion, from its elementary moral ideals and spiritual practice right on out to its most majestic and developed theology of Grace and Atonement, is aimed at one thing: to close the gap between God and man. Jesus Christ is the Mediator, the Daysman, between God and ourselves. But all who follow in His steps become little mediators, human daysmen, helping to close the gap between the human and the divine, between ourselves as we are and ourselves as God wants us to be, between man and God.

IV

The Turning Point

THOREAU SAID that "the mass of men live lives of quiet desperation."[1] The psychoanalysts tell us that there is at the bottom of our lives a "basic anxiety."[2] I believe that this "basic anxiety" may be akin to the spark of life itself, and may have been put within us to keep us from becoming too much like vegetables or dead fish. But unless this "basic anxiety" finds some adequate outlet and satisfaction, it causes us to live lives of "quiet desperation"—and sometimes not too quiet, either. Many people eat and sleep overmuch as a compensation for it. Some use their work as a refuge from it, giving much more detailed labor and much more over-time than the situation demands, because the hours alone or unoccupied give too good a chance for the "basic anxiety" to become a conscious craving for something which they cannot quite describe. Food, sleep, sex, pleasure, occupation—none of them are quite what we really want; and sooner or later we find it out. Life is for many people a series of experiments to get away from themselves, to resolve the "basic anxiety."

The people who seem to come nearest to resolving the conflict are the people with genuine religious faith. The greatest need is for some satisfying center round which to gather the many fragmentary elements of our emotions. We are not a clear-cut mixture, with a well-defined 'better

[1] "Economy" in *Walden.*
[2] Dr. Karen Horney, *The Neurotic Personality of Our Time.*

self' and a well-defined 'lower self,' though we recognize
the validity of that distinction. Rather, as Nicodemus says
in *Midnight Hour*,[3] "It is not a case of 'dual' but of mul-
tiple personality. A man contains, not only a Dr. Jekyll and
a Mr. Hyde, but often in the compass of one generic personality a saint and a devil, a believer and sceptic, a lover
and a cynic, an artist and a man of affairs, an enthusiast
and a critic and as many other selves as he may have rôles
in life." If anything can bring unity out of this diversity,
order out of this chaos—if anything can hitch these numer-
ous ribs to some coördinating spine, it must be something
which has immense power and which yet draws rather
than drives us to accept its primacy.

Perhaps we never recognize human nature in the raw so
much as when we see ourselves or others clinging for dear
life to the foul but warm nest where we may continue to
indulge the immaturity of unfaced conflicts. War itself does
not reveal so much human 'depravity' as this; nor does it
take more courage to face the fire of the enemy than really
to stir our emotional stumps and root up the comfortable
habits of feeling, thinking and acting, which keep us all
our lives living at about a quarter of our potential. Who-
ever can stir us from this deep-seated lethargy, this unwillingness to change, and give us an adequate alternative
to self-centeredness, will do us the greatest kindness that
can be done.

It is, I think, a psychological fact that we actually can
have only two possible centers for our basic emotion: ourselves, or God. Nothing else but God is big enough to
challenge the overwhelming claims of our own ego: no-
where else is there power to draw from us the intense love
which is ordinarily poured out upon ourselves. We may
think that another person whom we deeply love, or even
work in which we are tremendously interested, will fulfil

[3] p. 35.

this rôle for us; but there is a good deal of the projection of ego in much human love, and our work is almost wholly the 'lengthened shadow' of ourselves. People and interests fail us, the sense of their value fluctuates, their power to hold us flags. Not so with God. Once let a human being come under the power of the love of God, so that the divine love first extended towards us creates in us a love toward Him—once let a man be swept by the fire of the passion to find and do the will of God—and that man has begun to be lifted beyond himself. You see, God *remains:* He is there no matter what our emotions do, no matter how we fail Him or disobey Him—He is constant—and it is this which makes of religious faith such a powerful anchor in all the emotional storms which we experience.

Dr. John R. Mott says that the will of God was Jesus' "north star." To that His compass kept pointing. To that our compasses can be set, if we will set them. The will of God is vast, and as it concerns the whole universe and the whole future, it is of course in its totality beyond our knowing. But we learn something of the will of God as we study the Bible, and human history, and the lives of great believers and servants of humanity. We learn something of the will of God when we consult our consciences, when we pray and ask God to show us that portion of the will of God which is our special field, and then wait in prayer so as to give Him a chance to do it. God has a will for our vocation, which gives us a little piece of His will to fulfil. He has a will for our being married or single, if we will consult Him and not merely the strength of our own fears or desires. God has a will for every life, and for every hour of that life. If everyone were doing the will of God, we should find that the pieces of accomplishment fitted together in a perfect mosaic, like a vast puzzle being put together. The will of God is His blue print for creation. The plan is all right: the only slip occurs in the carrying out of the plan. If a pack of carpenters and plumbers get their heads together and decide the architect had the wrong idea about how to build the house, you will get a strange building. When we substitute our own wills for the will of God, we get a strange world.

The saving crisis of a human life is the place where we accept the will of God in place of our own wills, where we surrender our wills to Him. Everyone who begins even to suspect that there is a God knows that the outcome of believing in God must be the surrender of themselves to Him. This sometimes causes strong resistance and delay. A man with immense courage who was given the Croix de Guerre in the first world-war never had the courage to face the will of God, though he was fascinated with the ideas of it and played about the edge of it for a long time. This can be the only meaning of that rather terrible word, "It is a fearful thing to fall into the hands of the living God"[4]—fearful, i.e., to the old self, fearful to anyone who wants to have God and yet keep on having his own way.

But what is this surrender to God? It is more than an emotional lunge in His direction. It is a deliberate, systematic decision to have done with all that in life which denies or disobeys God, and to take on His full will for us so far as we can learn it. This means concretely the removal of whatever we know to be contrary to His will. And in order to know what these things may be, we need help in taking a *moral inventory* of our lives. It is possible for us when we do not feel well, or when we think it wise for any reason, to go to a doctor or a hospital and have a thorough physical check-up. Ministers and all trained spiritual and psychological workers ought to be able to help people to find a moral and spiritual check-up.

Take the Ten Commandments to begin with: read them over, and write down every place where one of them puts a

[4] Hebrews 10:31.

nick in your conscience. Or take a list of sins such as St.
Paul sets down in Romans 1, and in most of his Epistles,
and do the same thing. Or take the Sermon on the Mount,
more searching than any other statement of God's will for
man. Many have been helped by Dr. Robert E. Speer's dis-
tillation of the chief points of the Sermon on the Mount:
Absolute Honesty, Absolute Purity, Absolute Unselfish-
ness and Absolute Love. It will probably help if you can
find someone who knows life and people and the Christian
religion, and will sit down with you and help you to analyze
yourself and see what are your needs. For often we do not
see ourselves clearly; and such a performance as we are
suggesting, if we do it in a businesslike way with a view to
getting on to the next steps, may reveal an intense self-ab-
sorption in us that had not occurred to us at all! Basic fear,
basic pride, basic demand for sex, basic desire for security,
may lie deeper down than any of the 'sins' we are ac-
customed to see in the mirror of these scriptural passages.
Be quite simple and practical about this, very honest with
yourself, and do not dispute nor argue too much with yourself about whether something is all right or is not: remember "doubtful linen is dirty linen," and give yourself
a margin between you and wrong.

And then what? Then, either by yourself, or with the
help of a human witness, give yourself wholly to God.
Make a little ceremony of it if this will help to fix the importance and reality of the decision, by going to a church
and deciding before the altar. Get down on your knees.
Pray aloud, framing your desires into words, and your
words into consecutive sentences, so that there is no reservation and no hesitation and no question about the
finality of the gift of yourself to God. If another person is
with you, it is like a witness on a legal act, and the act of
praying before another person aloud will strengthen your
will and banish your self-consciousness. Ask for forgive-

ness, 'let go' completely inside so that no reservation lingers
about anything, and tell God all you feel. Note that this is
a matter of the *will,* not the emotions. For some, such an
experience is full of emotion; for others it is as cool as
signing over a house to someone else: the emotion is a
matter of personal temperament, but the act of will is universal.

But suppose our faith in God is very shaky—how can
we surrender to Him? Then we need to surrender to the
nearest thing to God that we know, as a preliminary to
finding Him. We must surrender to the God we see in
others, and it is entirely in order for us to do this, and to
walk for a while with this crutch. A drunken wastrel
having had no religious training nor knowledge whatever
in his entire life, met a man he thought was dead,— transformed, well-dressed,—and heard him witness to what
Christ had done for him. They had been drunk together
many a time; but one of them had found something. And
the other wanted what he saw. So that night he gave himself to what-he-saw-in-the-other-man; and through that
instrument, God came to him till he learned Who He is,
and what the power was that had changed his friend. We
must help people to begin way up-stream with only a rudi-
mentary desire for faith. A business man who had lost
everything and was jittery about the future prayed simply,
"O God, if there be a God, send me help now because I
need it." God answered that prayer. He will answer any
sincere prayer, however selfish, if the pray-er is willing to
move on up and out of his selfishness. If God is more
anxious to touch these people than they are to be touched,
we may be quite sure that any sincere reaching-out towards
Him will be met far more than half way. ". . . when he
was yet a great way off, his father saw him and ran . . ."*
That is always the picture of God, coming out to meet

* St. Luke 15:20.

every son returning from the far country, whether his fare out there was 'riotous living' or just the boredom of existence without God.

There is a truth which we need to learn well and to get down deep in our bones if we are to help people: and that is the truth contained in the verse St. John 7:17: "If any man willeth to do His will, he shall know of the doctrine." So often we think that if we knew God, we should live a good life. This says, Live a good life, and you will know God! The attempt really to be rid of our sins seems to open us to the God Who hovers over us with love all the time, and the readiness to stay in our sins seems to blind us to His Presence and make it impossible to believe that He exists. Says the Spanish philosopher, Unamuno, in a very great book called *The Tragic Sense of Life*[5] (anything but a tragic book!) "For God goes out to meet him who seeks Him with love and by love, and hides Himself from him who searches for Him with the cold and loveless reason. God wills that the heart should have rest, but not the head, reversing the order of the physical life in which the head sleeps and rests at times while the heart wakes and works unceasingly. And thus knowledge without love leads us away from God; and love, even without knowledge, and perhaps better without it, leads us to God, and through God to wisdom. Blessed are the pure in heart, for they shall see God!"

We shall find that man does not change his own heart, God changes his heart. But I have emphasized the human element in self-surrender because I believe there are countless people who have never had a decisive spiritual experience for the reason that no one has showed them where they might themselves lay hold of it. Someone said truly, "We take hold of God by the handle of our sins." When we see them clearly, and ask for forgiveness for them, and

[5] p. 194.

give over our wills to Him, we find Him. He is there. He has been there all along—only our sins have blinded us to Him, have made us even to disbelieve in His existence. The major work in the change of a human heart is God's work. It is the work of Grace. No man can change himself. But the two essential things to remember are (1) that God will not change a man against his will, and (2) that God always accepts those who turn to Him in penitence. In this sense, we each have a part in this decisive spiritual experience which marks the turning-point of human lives in relation to God.

Now this experience is what is meant by *conversion*. Essentially it comes about as a result of exposure to something hitherto unfamiliar or unaccepted. William Lyon Phelps showed how something very like conversion happens in other areas of life. Up until the age of twenty he intensely disliked good music—all he liked were comic operas and brass bands. When Theodore Thomas came to New Haven with a large orchestra, someone prevailed upon Phelps to go and listen. The program was Beethoven and Wagner. "Never shall I forget," he writes, "the boredom of that evening. I really suffered. It was genuine agony and distress. I gazed idly over the audience to see how my fellow-sufferers were enduring it. Some of them were asleep. How I envied them! The hideous noises were going ahead on the stage but these blissful souls were free from pain." Then he goes on: "Thinking it over after the concert I said to myself. Well maybe it's not my fault: maybe I ought to give it another try. So I went again. It wasn't quite so bad but almost. I was perfectly wretched. But fortunately for me I kept on going. And after a while I began to see rifts in the clouds, light in the darkness. And today I had rather hear a competent orchestra play Beethoven and Wagner than hear anything else in the world. I have become a discriminating lover of the best music. It gives me keen and exquisite delight. No music is too classical. The stiffer the program the better." There will be many who, in the spiritual life, need more than one exposure, need to "give it another try." And this applies, not more to those who consider themselves beyond the pale of religious experience or belief, than to those so long exposed to a rather mild form of religion that the really vital experience has never come to them. They need to find something much more vital than ordinary church routine, and "give it another try."

I do not think that anyone ever surrendered himself to all he believed about God, without finding God in the process. When the drag of sin is lost in the cry for forgiveness, when the reason drops its little brittle activity in the face of the mighty truth of the Great Presence, when the weary, frightened, bewildered spirit calms down in the hand of God as a wounded bird slowly does in a friendly human hand that means kindness, something steals over the total frame and emotions that can only be called *assurance*. Here there are no questions, for all is Answer— no doubts for all is Faith—no conflicts for all is Peace. As Masefield says in "The Everlasting Mercy,"[6]

> "I did not think, I did not strive,
>   The deep peace burnt my me alive;
>   The bolted door had broken in,
>   I knew that I had done with sin.
>   I knew that Christ had given me birth
>   To brother all the souls on earth,
>   And every bird and every beast
>   Should share the crumbs broke at the feast."

I must, however, enter a word of caution concerning conversion and the mentally or emotionally upset or unstable. It is such a tremendous thing, conversion,—so ob-

[6] p. 78.

viously the work and miracle of God,—that those who first begin to realize its almost magic powers believe that it can be the immediate solution to everything. For this reason, they are likely to hold it out before those troubled in mind and spirit with some kind of real sickness, as a sure and rapid cure. Sure, yes: but rapid, no. We must assist these people out of their difficulties, as we have said before, in two ways: helping them to begin to get well; and helping them to face the full Christian challenge and solution. So long as they are badly in the grip of 'nerves' or serious conflict, they are not sufficiently in possession of their inner faculties to make a long-range decision. One who is for any reason excited can easily be induced to take the step, and will greatly enjoy the drama of it: but it will be bad for him, because the step cannot hold, and the subsequent let-down and failure will bring more harm than help. It is often said, and with some truth, that conversion is not one big step, but a series of steps: but this is certainly true for the disturbed, the unstable, the neurotic. For them, all they can grasp of real conversion is to take the next step in responsibility, in maturity, that confronts them. They grow by this. They get well by this. They find God by this. It takes more time and patience; but anyone dealing with mentality or emotionally distressed people must be prepared to take time for them.

Conversion, the initial Christian decision, must not be tested by any psychological pattern: it must be tested on rather a broad basis by its fruits. We are not set to put people through certain psychological hoops: we are set to help liberate them from themselves into "the glorious liberty of the children of God." Some have been 'converted' who would wholly repudiate the word, and heartily deny that they were so good as this implies. But the test is in its effects. Where there is emerging victory over self-centered habits, where faith and its practise grow stronger, where the whole life bears a new tone, where human relationships come straighter, where work is better and more happily done, and where the Spirit of Christ affects one's relationships and affairs, there you have the footprints of Christ's wonderful work in conversion. If there have been real wrongs done to others, these must be made right by restitution—we cannot have bills unpaid, broken relations unmended, even ordinary loss of temper not apologized for, if we are to grow in strength. We know no such thing as complete victory without lapses; all we can do is to make use of the means God gives us to lessen their frequency and give us the courage to start again. There can and there will be steady growth when we keep depending on God, and making use of the ways He offers us to grow in the new life.

All this, I must point out, is essentially a religious and not merely a psychological experience. Psychology has scarcely any counterpart to it. Psychology knows certain sudden, sometimes lasting, changes in the human psyche, and let us be thankful for everything that helps men upward. But it knows nothing of forgiveness, yet forgiveness is the only real break between us and the past. We cannot find in psychology anything approaching atonement, though psychology itself must recognize how deep in human beings is the longing for something to *make up for* their sins as they certainly cannot do for themselves. The 'good life,' however good and however much we want it, has no drawing-power in it like the love of God. And no study or understanding of the laws of psychology can possibly offer us anything of the help that is indicated by the word 'grace.' Therefore, while psychology can describe the experiences of religion, it cannot offer the dynamic to produce them, as Harold Begbie observed long ago.[7]

Do you say that personal conversion is upon too small

[7] *Twice-Born Men.*

a scale to matter in this time of swirling revolution? There are two things to reply: the first is, that the rise of the ideologies in our time is just one long tragic instance of the conversion of individuals to the wrong thing upon a scale perhaps never before seen in history, a kind of conversion backwards and by coercion which has had most awful consequences; the second is, that unless we make conversion to the great Christian realities the business of all men of good will, there is nothing to prevent the fresh rise of human ideologies working by coercion to do even more harm than has been done to date—and Christian conversion can only be the willing conversion of individual men. There seems to be within men and within mankind an empty pool of need which can be artificially filled with the content of guilt and weakness and so played upon by anything which promises leadership and collective security, or which can be filled with the content of forgiveness and strength and so become a reservoir of Christian grace for the man and for his world. The vast totalitarian schemes had their rise just at a time when the Christian Church had become too self-conscious, too insistent about the intellectual and social aspects of Christianity, too eager to trail the latest pronouncement of 'science,' to see to it that the average range of men met its chief challenge and dynamic in some attractive and available form. We were too 'tolerant' to engage in 'propaganda' based upon the faith that "the head of every man is Christ." Satan, however, was not so scrupulous: he was busy all the time getting across his ideas about conversion and the bringing of the world under a very difficult "head" from Christ. While the ecclesiastical technicians dealt with fine niceties, while many clergy were a good deal more like boys 'playing church' than like prophets giving the Word of God to man, these horrible monstrous ideas bred and spread till the world has been seared and scalded with their breath.

The Turning Point

There is no choice between any of them: the choice is between all of them on one side, and Christianity on the other. Jacques Maritain says, "The present war gives us notice that the world has done with neutrality. Willingly or unwillingly, States will be obliged to make a choice for or against the Gospel. They will be shaped either by the totalitarian spirit or by the Christian spirit."[8] Obviously, states cannot joint directly in the propaganda of the tenets of any one faith: but they can recognize that their own welfare and continuance depend upon the creation of men and women that believe in God and try to do what He tells them; they can help, and refuse to hinder, those who make such results their aim. Therefore the helping of individuals by the teaching and contagion of faith is one of the very greatest services that can be performed for the nation, and for the peace of the world.

I close with the story of how the "turning point" came in the life of a Canadian business man. He is a man of fine family background, successful in business, whose vague feelings of futility came somewhat to a head when his son went overseas in the war, and he realized that he was "somehow responsible for the world's awful mess." For many years, the minister of the church to which he nominally belonged had sought to help him find the reality of spiritual faith, but without success. A couple of years ago they met on a vacation, and he told the minister he was more open to what he had to say. It still took some time for it to ferment; but finally, he says, "I came to the conclusion that I would have to set my whole house in order. I decided to take the approaching Lenten season to 'condition myself' for a full commitment to God. My parson encouraged me with some stories of others who had taken this step, and he enabled me to meet several of them. I was certainly impressed by them and their experiences. During

[8] *The Rights of Man and Natural Law,* p. 23.

Lent I prayed earnestly, but I must admit not without some embarrassment and sense of artificiality. I started to read the Bible, and attempted to set up a daily habit of prayer. I must say that I went about all this with *little enthusiasm!* My approach to the whole proposition of surrender was about as spirited as preparing to go into the hospital for an operation—practical, but apprehensive.

"After this 'conditioning process,' I made an appointment with the parson and in prayer with him I committed my life wholly to Christ. It was a premeditated, deliberate decision, with little apparent, immediate result.

"One immediate, concrete, and surprising result was the ease with which I was able to give up smoking. I had tried again and again to give it up, and always with the same result—really exhausting moral battle, with myself ever the battered loser. My experience this time was utterly different. Whereas in the past there had always been a constant moral struggle—'shall I or shall I not'—there was this time a complete absence of any such agony over the issue, and consequently no difficulty about carrying it through.

"I made my commitment on March 13, 1944. For the first few months I felt like a person whose vaccination has not taken. My parson assured me, however, that the new life was not essentially one of feeling, but mainly one of fact and faith. Feelings one way or the other were incidental. After nine months, I realize that he was right, and that God has honored my initial decision in the following ways:

"The former feeling of futility and frustration has gone

"A certain nervous tension under which I have lived and worked of late years has also disappeared.

"I am a much more sociable person, as a number of my friends have noticed—this, I may say, is in marked contrast with my former disposition.

The Turning Point

"My daily habit of prayer, Bible reading and meditation have, fortunately for me, continued out of a spontaneous desire, and as the weeks and months pass I am very conscious of the ever-increasing importance which this assumes in my life. Mention of these facts reminds me of a prediction which my spiritual mentor made to me early last year. He wrote to me saying, 'I feel I can predict for you a new sense of real pleasure, of a spiritual kind, that you have never known, in prayers and meditations. I guarantee this, however extraordinary you may now think it to be.'

"I go to church now with keenness, and am finding real satisfaction and needed comfort in public worship.

"There has come a distinct sharpening of my moral convictions, and a somewhat startling awakening of conscience. This phase of my new life seems to me the most realistic of all. No matter what doubts may occasionally arise as to the reality of this new experience, in certain respects, I need no proof that my own moral and spiritual life is undergoing a drastic change—almost, I am tempted to say, without much that I can do about it.

"Another surprising thing is that I find myself becoming involved in Christian work, and, what is more surprising, this brings me considerable satisfaction. I can see greater and greater possibilities opening up in this direction.

"My interest in Christian work through the Church began with a week-end which I spent in Calvary House last June. I found myself taking part in religious meetings for eight hours—in one day! This would have seemed most improbable if not impossible in the old days, but in June I found myself quite definitely interested. Upon returning home, I learned that the churches of my home town were planning to have Dr. E. Stanley Jones come to us for a week. I knew something of the remarkable spiritual awakening that had taken place in the life of Manchester, England, and my interest in such matters had been so aroused that I wrote to certain people in England to get all the information possible. This resulted in my taking a large part of the responsibility for organizing the business men of the town to lend their moral support to Dr. Jones and to the churches in a preaching mission. The results were extraordinarily successful.

"Prior to my Spiritual 'D-Day,' I was very little interested in the Church or Christian work generally. Relating the incident of my association with the city-wide mission under Dr. E. Stanley Jones caused me to realize, to my amazement, that in the ten months which have elapsed since my commitment I have been involved in, or been asked to take part in, no less than six separate programmes of a Christian character. The most recent, and by far the most important, is the suggestion that I now undertake the organization in my home town of a group of possibly five hundred Protestant laymen as part of the programme of the recently organized Canadian Council of Churches. A year ago any suggestion that I would ever find myself involved in such work as this would have seemed fantastic in the extreme. All of these opportunities have come to me without any sort of seeking on my part."

V

Understanding People

"THE ENTIRE WORLD is nothing in comparison with human personality, with the unique person of a man, with his unique fate. Man lives in an agony, and wants to know who he is, where he comes from and whither he is going." So speaks the Russian philosopher Nicolas Berdyaev,[1] pointing out to us the high evaluation, the intense concern and compassion for individuals which must be ours if we would help them; and also the real and deep problems, fundamentally religious, which confront people and which we, with all our limitation and unworthiness, must try to solve ourselves and help them to solve.

It is clear that we must always meet people with a will to understand them. We shall need to empty ourselves of obtrusive points of view, touchiness when some pet convictions may be challenged or stepped on, and any approximation of the rôle of moral monitor—these things will drive people from us and put them beyond our power to help. The French proverb *"tout a savoir c'est tout a pardonner"* is ethically loose; to know all is not to pardon all: but to know all *is* to understand all. If we are to understand people, we shall need to let ideas, beliefs, experiences to which we are personally strangers wash over us like waves. We shall learn to make ourselves outwardly unshockable though we be listening to something which is quite unfamiliar, or even a shock to our own moral con-

[1] *Slavery and Freedom*, p. 20.

victions. We must increasingly learn to get on board with any kind of person on earth—a shy little milk-sop that hasn't the courage to get into trouble, a bluff and confident business man, a roaring swaggering pagan, a saint, a pious church-pharisee, a sensitive artist or intellectual, a child, a criminal. Any one of them may need help, and we may be the people who should give it to them. An understanding heart is the greatest gift God can give to anyone—and by seeking, by learning and by prayer, an understanding heart can be cultivated. We need first of all, then, a large-hearted sympathy, comprehensive, inclusive and out-going.

Human life is like a car, with the body for a chassis, the emotions and will for an engine, and the mind and spirit for a driver. When all are working, and working together, we get where we are going with despatch and without mishap. But when there is trouble in any of these departments, there is a halt and maybe a break-down. The body has its needs: it craves food, warmth, use, affection. Insufficient sleep or exercise, lack of medical attention, want of proper food, or illness, can throw body and mind out of line. The mind affects the body, but the body also affects the mind. Sometimes people look for spiritual help when they ought to consult a good doctor first. Sometimes the difficulty is in the emotions, where there is a conflict between ego and sex, for example; or between duty and desire; or between private wishes and public decorum; or between two desires that cannot be carried out at the same time; or between a desire and a fear. Emotions cannot be located, like the heart or liver: but they affect the nerves, and are affected by them. Our physical health has improved enormously in the past quarter century; but perhaps our emotional health has declined, and there are great numbers of people who are in conflict, or fear, and when they meet a taxing situation they "can't take it." As the body and the emotions are constantly affecting one another, so does the human spirit constantly affect both body and emotions and it is in turn affected by them. If man "lives in an agony, and wants to know who he is, where he comes from and whither he is going," as Berdyaev says, he cannot find balm for the agony nor answers to his questions, either in his body or in his emotions; these high matters concern the nature of life itself. And if we seek human solutions to them, which are to be found in the unaided insight and strength of man himself, we shall be doomed to disappointment. They call for assistance from a yet higher sphere. All three of these areas, whatever their relation to each other, are pragmatic realities which anybody must accept who knows human life and human nature.

As man's range takes in the entire sweep from the simplest physical reactions to the highest of spiritual sacrifice, so we must be prepared to find everything within everybody. It is not that one is a saint, and the other is a sinner—obvious and clear-cut: there will be found enormous weaknesses in the holiest people in the world and things of which they are bitterly ashamed, and there will be found tremendous fineness sometimes in the most useless and even degraded people. "We are Legion," as the man with evil spirits said of himself. It is common to hear people put this truth in this way: 'we are not black or white, we are grey.' That is not quite the reality: we are not so much grey, which is mixed; we are checkered, with black and white alternating. Or perhaps more like patch-work, for the sections do not appear with any regularity, or any proportion. The problem in really helping people is to watch this strange mixture, in ourselves and in other people, and keep faith to believe that it is possible and worth-while to try to strengthen the best in people and to help them root out the worst. Over the long haul, that takes a lot of faith and a lot of courage. The best of people are often self-deceived. Any man can flip over in a second of time from overwhelming inferiority which reduces him inside to a whining baby, to over-weening conceit which makes him strut like a peacock; and then he can flip back again when his wife tells him he made a poor speech or the boss jumps him for a foolish mistake. If we are honest about ourselves, if we are realistic about life, human nature is something!

I do not know anything less than religious faith, which one has experienced within oneself, and which knows the inner witness to at least some of the "fruits of redemption," that can have any real hope about human nature. All the talk about the post-war world that hoped to bring Utopia on the scene the moment hell had left it was only talk and no more. The scotching of war from the human scene needs more than the rearrangement of man's politics and economics: it needs the change of man's heart. The number of people who are willing to let their hearts be changed is relatively small, though larger than some of us think. The likelihood of the thing happening on a very wide-spread basis is slim. Only our faith in God, and His power to transform men, will give us the confidence to believe that human nature can be re-made, and that the Kingdom can come on earth. Christianity—make no mistake about it— does not hold a high view of human nature: it holds a low one. It has any amount of faith about how much can happen to man when he lets God save him; but it has little hope for man as he is. We shall do a far better job of helping people if we adopt the two-fold Christian view of man at the outset: disillusionment about man as he is, great faith about man as he can be with the help of God.

These things should make us very tender and under-standing with actual, living people. The inner fight to express the 'self,' and the social demand to keep the self out of the way—the deep personal craving to create, to accomplish, to 'cut ice,' and the self-questioning that is ever-lastingly running athwart it—the conflicting emotions of overbearing self-importance and infinitesimal nothingness —the loveable humor and humanity and interesting ways of people, set over against their selfishness, meanness and boring mediocrity—these considerations which cause cynicism and despair in those who seek a merely human solution, and maybe the abandonment of seeking to help at all, constitute for those who believe in God and the Christian faith the great challenge to their love, their sympathy and their faith. Cynicism is the reaction of one group: compassion of the other. Jesus felt sorry for people. He said they were "like sheep without a shepherd."

What to do with the ego—that is the main problem. We must first meet it with sympathy and understanding as it comes towards us riding on the personality, let us say, of a new acquaintance. It may be an attractive ego, that draws people to it by happy qualities, and seems adequate to anything. It may be an uncertain and bashful ego, insecure, wondering whether a new acquaintance means a new bafflement or a new hurt. It may be the kind of ego we do not understand at all, that lives on a different axis in another world of interests. We want to mesh our gears if possible, and find something in common; there needs to be mutuality, and the experiment of interchange. We want to help that ego to be its real self, to find a healthy, happy expression of its fundamental urge to live. If we feel interest and congeniality, let this come out by touching gradually deeper levels of interchange. Without flattery, let us always be appreciative, for this draws forth the best in people, and we want to discover that best and encourage it. It will soon be evident to another person that we are interested in his 'soul' or his 'reformation,' unless we are honestly interested from the first in *him*—in the whole of him. Said Forbes Robinson,[2] "Sometimes I have been foolish enough to glory in the fact, and to think that I honour God in

[2] *Letters to His Friends*, p. 143.

caring only for my brother's soul and not for his whole life. But love has taught me that this is a low and incomplete view. God numbers the very hairs of our head, and he who loves and tries to help another must enter into his life and care for all that he cares for."

Most of us meet and mingle with people uncreatively—on a static instead of a dynamic basis. We just 'accept' them. We begin early in the game to pigeonhole them: "She's impossible," "He's a saint"—which means nothing can be done for the first, and nothing needs to be done for the second. As a matter of fact, neither of those things is strictly true: both need help, and both can be helped. When we love people, we are likely to err on the side of not being realistic about them, not wishing to raise points that create an issue or a challenge in a comfortable relationship. And when we dislike people, we are likely to be so realistic about them that we have no faith in what even God can do for them. Said Phillips Brooks, "It seems to me that a large part of the troubles and mistakes of our pastoral life comes from our having too high an estimate of men's present condition and too low an estimate of their possibility."[3] Rosy views that glorify people, dark views that put them beyond helping, indifferent views in the middle that will not trouble or bother—any one of these three is about as bad as the others.

We must by natural stages get down to a deeper level of reality with people. Sympathy and understanding come first, going out to them, *liking* them (for everybody likes to be liked, and people in the habit of liking people can multiply their likes almost without number, and quite sincerely, too). But helping people is a product of real friendship. We must understand human nature itself. We must understand this particular son of Adam that we met this morning in the office. If it is possible, and we feel drawn to do it, we

[3] *Lectures on Preaching,* p. 81.

want to help him. We may know he is in difficulty, we may know he is riding the crest of success, we may know nothing about him. I want to illustrate what I mean by a deeper knowledge of human nature, and of this particular individual, by running down one problem that we meet fairly often.

Let us take the problem of religious unbelief, indifference or doubt. A man has read some science, he looks back with contempt on the kind of religion he was taught in his youth, he believes in 'the Golden Rule' and the 'Sermon on the Mount' (so he says), and he does his share in the community. But he doesn't go to church—he doesn't pray or read his Bible often—because he doesn't "believe." He thinks that faith is wishful thinking: people believe because they want to believe. Does it ever occur to him that he disbelieves because that goes better with the kind of life he wants to live? It will be most unwise to try to answer his specific objections to, say the doctrine of the Virgin Birth, or the Trinity; for even if you answer one of his questions, he will move quickly to another, and the conversation will end on an argument. I am convinced that unbelief is born of these things:

a. Lack of information about the Christian faith.
b. Fear that faith would make us change our lives and ways.
c. Want of exposure to living faith, with resultant discouragement at finding it for ourselves.
d. Defeat in our own lives which makes faith impossible.

Most people who 'doubt' know very little about Christianity. If they are intellectually honest, see if you can get them to read a book like T. R. Glover's *The Jesus of History,* or some good standard life of Christ, or almost any of C. S. Lewis' books, or Elton Trueblood's *Predicament of Modern Man.* See if you can get him to read the Bible with a view to finding out what it says.

Many people are kept away from Christianity, not by cold logic, but by cold feet. They know that religion exercises a great sway, makes people do costly and unconventional things. They know that religion will not brook our prejudices, indulgences, our unbridled desire for our own way. Unbelief is a smoke-screen sometimes for sheer cowardice. We will not say such a thing to anyone in an accusing way, but in an explanatory way, preferably with a pinch of autobiography in it.

Again, many have never been exposed to anything more spiritually dynamic than an average church service. So often in church people are told what to do, but not *how* to do it. Many who come a few times are more in earnest than we realize; but there is no way to take hold of it for themselves. They give up, not from adequate intellectual reasons (they manufacture these later), but from despair at not being able themselves to find God. Doubt becomes then the rationalization of discouragement.

But for some, doubt is the direct result of defeat. A woman came saying she had lost her faith. The facts of her life were: she hated her husband and was miserable with him, she was filled with self-pity, worried over her children, thinking about divorce and perhaps suicide. Unbelief was for her the intellectualization of her emotional misery: it was the only thing that fitted the life she knew and was living. That is, it was purely emotional in origin. When she saw this, she began taking reasonable steps towards faith. Faith affects the way we live; but the way we live affects faith, too. Adequate, happy living goes with faith: inadequate, unhappy living breeds the emotions in which doubt is born.

Brought down to actualities, then, our friend who 'doesn't believe' needs to be helped to see himself and his questions in a new light. He needs more knowledge of the facts, more honesty in facing his real motives, more expo-

sure to the contagion of living faith, and the willingness
to live on a new and higher moral level where faith will
come more naturally. For unbelief is like a dark room. It
may be dark because the sun is not out and the skies are
cloudy. Or it may be dark because the windows are dirty.
We cannot sweep away the clouds, nor turn on the sun:
but we can wash the windows!

It makes all the difference how we make such facts as
these known to people. None of us likes to be exposed, or
'found out', least of all by anyone whom we have not come
to trust deeply. Therefore there must never be accusation
in the way we bring these things out, or anything like
cornering people. It is mightily important that at all times
the element of friendship, with its note of equality, should
be dominant in our relations to people. It is far better if
we can put the truth in a general form, or in terms of our
own experience, and let the other person come up with the
application to his own life. We need to be, as Henry Drummond said, "suggestive" rather than "dogmatic" at all
times. We need to give the appearance of feeling our way
with people, even if the ground is familiar to us: and we
can do this with total sincerity because this ground in his
particular experience is new ground to us. The whole experience is as if we were taking a walk together over his
country estate, to which he had invited us; and after we
arrived, he found we knew something about landscaping,
or farming, or dairying, or forestry, and we talked over
together what it was best to do as we walked along. It is
not a professional matter, though there may be some experience gained in a professional way. We are not there
to dogmatize, or order, or even advise: we are there as a
trusted, experienced friend who is free to make modest
suggestions, remembering that the estate is his, not ours.
This 'doing-it-together' is of the essense of helping people
in an understanding way.

How You Can Help Other People

Now in most lives there is an untold secret. Some old wound of love, some long-gone family tragedy, some deep frustration, some deep-seated resentment, some great hope or aspiration, some longing for great human service, some degrading habit that still persists though it be first spoken of as if it lay in the distant past, some ever-present sorrow —there is *something* in most people which they never tell, but would give almost anything if they could find the right person to tell, and from telling which there would result an emotional release that they crave. Sometimes to a total stranger we can say things we cannot say to our best friend, and casual acquaintances on trains, etc. will often pour out their hearts. If we know how to draw them out little by little, they may blurt out the real thing that is on their minds. But only if they come to (1) trust us as persons, and (2) know that what they say will be kept in strictest confidence. Very seldom do these deep personal revelations come forth under the pressure of curiosity or direct questions: it takes a poultice to draw them out, and the poultice is sympathetic listening while they come nearer and nearer to the thing they would like to say. The most we can do is to say something like this: "Do you think we have gotten to the bottom of your needs?" or "Is there anything else you think ought to come out?", and then perhaps be willing to tell of the release that came when we were at last honest ourselves about the realest need in our lives. We must keep from anything like coercion in all this, letting the urge come from within the person himself. Gamaliel Bradford knew the human heart, and it was his judgment that, "To confide one's troubles, griefs, and sufferings, to confide one's triumphs and hopes, to confide one's life experience of all sorts, this is an unquenchable, an irresistible longing, from which no one is altogether free, and which when it is repressed in one form, is sure to manifest itself in another."[4]

[4] *Life and I,* Gamaliel Bradford, p. 255.

Understanding People

Dr. Karl DeSchweinitz emphasizes the need in people to reveal themselves to others and to seek help by doing so. "It is," he says, ". . . the unusual man who is able to resist the desire to unburden himself, and frequently the price of resistance is a miserable and embittered personality. People want to tell. When they hesitate, it is only because they wish to be certain that they have found an individual in whom with security they can confide. And by security they mean, not merely safety from a repetition to others of what they have told or the assurance of action that can be taken to help them, but also the far greater security that comes from the knowledge that they are understood, for people seem almost instinctively to believe, and rightly, that the individual who understands them will guard their secrets and will be able to advise them. . . . Most people want to unburden themselves of the things that are troubling them. The person in difficulty may share his secret in part here and in part there, or he may select someone to whom he reveals the whole story. In one way or another he will seek to relieve himself of the load he has been carrying. All he asks is that his confident be a person who will understand him and with whom he can feel secure."[5]

Human nature is, I think, more varied than it is complex. This means for our purposes that we need infinite tact and sympathy in getting on the inside of people, in understanding their problem and what they think of their problem; but once we have established a real and understanding relation, the solution of the problem along Christian lines in not impossibly complicated. It often takes much more of simple honesty and courage than it takes of technical knowledge of any kind or profound understanding. I am constantly amazed, not at how much it takes to move and help people, but at how little. We get close to a difficulty which

[5] Karl De Schweinitz, *The Art of Helping People Out of Trouble*, Houghton Mifflin Company, pp. 61 and 76.

seems insurmountable to the person who is in it: we set about with love and insight and faith to get at the bottom of it, and find it is as if we had taken a stick of dynamite to blow out a rock in a field which is not buried two feet deep. I am not saying there are not very real complicated situations which confront people: I am saying that these go back to rather simple mistakes, easily discovered wrong values, and often stem from one big thing, like fear or resentment which once fully faced begins to unravel the whole difficulty. If there be an answer to the problem of human life, it must be a relatively simple answer, else it would not be available for the vast majority of people. The application of Christianity to life is largely a matter of being *willing* to start. We often sin ourselves into complexity; we shall get ourselves out by simplicity. Says Hocking, "Subtle religion is always false religion."

The deepest thing I believe about human nature is that God has created us with an image of Christ within us. The animal is there, to be sure, with all the force of sheer instinctive urges. But there is something else there that is as pervasive as instinct; and that is spiritual hunger and capacity which is amazingly satisfied by Christ. St. John says there is an organic connection between Him and all of us: "That was the true light which lighteth every man. . ." This means there is a working identity between Christ and our own consciences. An ignorant woman of the bush in Africa heard the preaching of a Christian God, and said to someone, "There, I always told you there must be a God like that!" Where does that recognition of familiarity come from, as if this great Outsider Who comes to us were already an Insider? I believe that God has left within us a vacant space which Christ exactly fills. That space is sometimes filled by usurpers and counterfeits, but they do not fit it: only Christ exactly fits and fills and satisfies that empty space within us. God put it there, that the Christ without might be recognized by the Christ within.

It is not our rôle to manage people, but to help them. This really means to help them help themselves. Most of them do not understand life and how it works, and will not until faith becomes real to them. To this end, we must help people understand themselves by revealing them to themselves. The real problem, the real motive, the real sin back of the problem, the real desire that is ruling them,—we must find this. It must be done without censure or blame, without saying too little or too much, with sympathy, humour, concern and great expectation. Francis Thompson tells in his Life of St. Ignatius Loyola of one who heard the Jesuits preach at Coimbra, and read the *Exercises*,[6] and was asked, "Did they not show you monsters or devils?" The charge was that the Jesuits were magicians. "Worse than that," said he, "they showed me myself." That must always be our aim.

The deepest concern in all men is what is going to happen to them. The wrong solution for that concern is simple egotism: "my life is mine, and I will have my way." Berdyaev says that "The fall of man finds expression most of all in the fact that he is a tyrant. He is a tyrant, if not on a great scale, then on a small, if not in the state, if not in the pages of world history, then in his family, in his shop, in his office, in the bureaucratic establishment in which he occupies the very smallest position."[7] We know how true that is, how true it is of *us,* how the world hated Hitler not alone for the evil he did but because at bottom we are all so much like him in the thrust of ego! Now when the fears of the ego are dissolved in faith, when the ambitions of the ego are lost in the great cause of faith in the world,

[6] p. 159.
[7] *Slavery and Freedom*, p. 61.

when the longing of the ego for company and association is taken up in the reality of fellowship with others who share the same faith and work in the same cause, then the imperious ego really finds what all along it has sought.

But the understanding of people comes by love, by sympathy, by entering into their lives. There is so much general interest in people which has no creative outlet, and comes out in gossip and 'personalities'—I know someone with a positive passion to spread *correct* gossip, to set people straight who have spread incorrect gossip! What a 'natural' to help people if that interest were lifted up and made positive and creative, through responsible understanding! How much criticalness of people is meant to be turned into the same kind of responsible understanding! What would it do for the world if there were released into it large numbers of understanding people with power to help?

VI

What Fellowship Does

IT IS IMPOSSIBLE to help anyone 'in himself,' without helping him also in his human relationships : for we cannot live
a full life apart from other people. Says Dr. Alexander
Reid Martin, "Psychiatric emphasis is shifting from what
goes on inside the individual to what goes on between
individuals." The very picture of abnormality, and of
unhappiness, is loneliness. And there is a great deal of
it today. The mere presence of many people is no guarantee against it : you can feel more lonely sitting in a
theatre surrounded by people, or going to a football
game by yourself, than when you are alone in your own
room. We probably see more faces and hear more voices
and know more names than any generation that ever lived ;
but the very number of acquaintances makes for super-
ficiality. Back of much of the domestic unhappiness and
divorce lies an incapacity for deep, long-range relationships : we squeeze people like oranges for the juice that is
in them for us, and throw them aside. Part of the sickness
of our time is the shallowness, impermanence, unsatisfac-
toriness of our human relations. There can be no rebuilding of man or society today unless there is also a rebuilding
of relationships.

There is a very remarkable book by Martin Buber, called
I and Thou, the theme of which is that "all true life is
meeting." We do not function, we do not live, apart from
the people with whom we are in contact. Every step away

from the self-centeredness which lies so close to neuroticism
that it often passes over into it, must be a step towards
God and also a step towards people. Out of the narrowing
circle of self, with its limited world and its monotonous
round, with its fears and its love for what it can control, a
prisoned life ventures forth, steps into the circle of another
life, discovers another round, another self with fears and
hungers for real human contact, meets there a world it cannot control, and by beginning to lose itself in the world of
another begins to find itself. The kind of self which uses
others as 'things' makes them merely the extension of its
own self-centeredness, and by so much cuts off its own
growth. The more other people a man can live himself into,
the larger the orbit and potential of his life: and the
healthier are his emotions likely to be.

There are three levels of our meeting with other people.
The first is where they are merely *objects*—workmen whose
sweat and muscle support us by what they do in far-off
mines, people who serve us at arm's length in stores, on
subways, or closer to home, people with whom we meet
but do not mesh, animated machines, things with brains in
them. The second is where people are *objects emotionally
needful to us*—bridge-table friends who while away an
afternoon that would be deadly alone, people on whom we
have grown dependent for any reason, people whose affections feed ours, people whom in a business, or social, or
professional, or sexual, way we *use* for the pleasure or
profit they bring to us. The third is where people *become
people* to us—where they are ends, not means, where their
life becomes important to us, its enrichment, its fullness,
its greatest possible creative development, become part of
our joy and part of our responsibility. We all need people
and to some degree have to have them, but when we find
ourselves tending to use people for our own ends, contrary to the development of their own proper objectives,

then we are spoiling the relationship. Only when men are ends to each other are they free men : only in such relationships as exist between these free men can true fellowship be said to exist. For a fellow is precisely an equal.

Here is where spiritual fellowship becomes so immensely important in democracies. Men are not 'created equal' in their talents, nor in their personalities, nor in their qualities of service : they are 'created equal' in their rights before the law, and in their worth before God. We all know that the simple goodness of an unlettered peasant may stand much higher before God than the self-conscious spiritual efforts of a highly trained intellectual. When it comes to spiritual gifts, insight, devotion, power, there is no one class, race or group of people with any copyright on an exclusive access to them. An ignorant man that loves Christ, a child that knows Him, may say the telling thing, or do the needful thing, better than anyone else. We know all this 'theoretically :' but we see it, we experience it, when we come into a true Christian fellowship where human distinctions give way before the one vast distinction between those who are led by the Spirit of God and those who are not.

Our whole feeling about the worth of Negroes, for instance, is lifted when a Negro man talks simply in a meeting about the way Christ has taken prejudice and bitterness from his heart : we cannot refuse fellowship to him, he has himself created it by the fineness of his own spirit. A labor leader who might start hostile emotions in an industrialist tells of what Christ means to him as a Friend and a Guide, and how he believes that in Him are to be reconciled the interests of labor and management : this begets fellowship, a heightened confidence of what Christian fellowship can mean as a cement to create human solidarity. A Jew who knows now the fullness of Christian experience, and is ready to give the humblest service, and lives in the most generous way towards people, and draws people to his

Lord by his own humility and self-effacement—such a man cuts the prejudice from your heart when you meet and know him in the flesh.

We realize that God meant America to be a great melting-pot; but this will only take place as all these separate individual particles that go to make up this amazing melee are themselves sound, healthy, coöperative people. Many people have a sentimental, emotional idea of "brotherhood," but forget that brotherhood means that *some men become brothers* who were not brothers before. Living, organic, human relationships existing, not between abstractions, but between actual human beings—these are the stuff of which real democracy can alone be built. Richard Russell says, "The rebuilding of Europe cannot now be political; political faiths can no longer move the hearts and spirits of men. . . . The Europe of the future will be built upon these little communities or brotherhoods. . . The Christian minority can alone rebuild Europe."[1]

Recently there was a meeting to which there happened to come a very diverse group of men. There were two Jews, two Negroes, two union men, two industrialists, two parsons, two laymen, two Hungarians, a Greek, a Russian, a Swiss, a chemist, a missionary from India. What could draw together such a company? Just the word getting round that there were power and fellowship to be found there. One by one the stories were recounted, how this one found help in prayer, how another was transformed when drink had him in its grip, how another was finding Christ the solution in modern industry. There was a quietness throughout—nobody was preaching, nobody was attempting to gain or hold the stage, each one spoke as if he were speaking *for* as well as *to* the rest of the company, an atmosphere of perfect freedom and quiet, refreshing love pervaded the place. A Negro arose who said he had to go

[1] Quoted F. Noel Palmer, *Christ's Way With People,* p. 19.

early—he is a college teacher and a former well-known athlete: what he said was this, "I have no religious faith of my own. My father was a minister, but I have reacted against it all. But what I have seen and heard here today, these things spoken by such diverse types of men, in such perfect openness and freedom, gives me a new faith that the principles of Christ may yet prove to be the basis of human unity." He was back soon at another meeting, and said, "I don't know what draws me here, but I feel a spirit here that I have never felt anywhere else."

It is to me very clear that if this man had met each one of those thirty men singly, and singly heard their story, he might have been moved by it: but what really moved him in the meeting was these men *in fellowship with one another*. It was not only the lives that were impressive: it was rather the relationships that were impressive. Here is something for us to ponder and to investigate. It reminds us of the wonderful word from Robert Barclay, one of the early theologians of the Quakers, where he describes his first meeting with them: "Not by strength of arguments or by a particular disquisition of each doctrine, and a convincement of my understanding thereby, came I to receive and bear witness of the Truth, but by being secretly reached by the Life. For, when I came into the silent assemblies of God's people, I felt a secret power among them, which touched my heart; and as I gave way to it I found the evil weakening in me and the good raised up . . . and indeed this is the surest way to become a Christian." [2]

So much of our real malady today lies in our relationships. So often in our relations, we fear, and use, and resist, and fight, and dominate, when we ought to trust, and cooperate, and lay ourselves open, and work in teamwork. Whatever is to offer us the solution must offer us something else besides pure individualism at one end, and the

[2] *William Penn,* Vulliamy, pp. 126-7.

terrible travesties of fellowship represented by various political and economic 'collectivisms' at the other. *We must learn the art of fellowship.* Nothing else picks up the need of the individual to find himself in relation to a group, and nothing else can prevent the group from dominating or using him, except some training in the free fellowship which exists between people who meet in and under God.

We must get all this beyond the mere natural gregariousness of man. We are gregarious. Life is lonely in the deep country, so we swarm in town. Life is full of suffering and disappointment, but a good round of gossip with a neighbour relieves it considerably. As Romain Rolland said, "The herd is evil-smelling, but it gives warmth." There is a false kind of fellowship-for-fellowship's-sake that is to be avoided. Jacques Maritain tells us that "the Germanic notion of community is built on a nostalgic longing to be together, on the emotional need for communion for its own sake—fusion within the community thus becomes a compensation for an abnormal feeling of loneliness and distress."[3] When any of us join something for the mere sake of "belonging," instead of to link ourselves together with others for the accomplishment of a common purpose, we have begun with a selfish attitude which is itself the very negation of the fellowship we think we seek. We shall find that we can never get fellowship except by giving it.

The roadway to fellowship for most of us lies in the development of one honest, loving, free relationship with some other person. When another is used of God to bring faith to us, and we find we can open our hearts to him, he is likely to be a doorway into other such relationships, i.e. fellowship. The company to which he belongs is likely to become our company, too.

The Christian movement was like this in the beginning. Jesus called individual men to follow Him, but they did it

[3] *The Rights of Man and Natural Law,* p. 40.

in a company and in fact they were never again mere individuals. When they accepted His call and His challenge, they accepted also His cause and His company. The mystical reality of the Christian company was seen on the day of Pentecost when they were gathered together "with one accord in one place" and the Spirit of God came mightily upon them, both drawing out their individual capacities and also deepening their corporate life.[4] The church in that day was much less an institution with customs and organizations and officers, then a spiritual family. Their meetings were a cross between a modern church service and a testimony meeting. Dr. E. F. Scott, one of the scholarly authorities on the New Testament and the early church, says, "The exercise of the spiritual gifts was thus the characteristic element in the primitive worship. Those gifts might vary in their nature and degree according to the capacity of each individual, but they were bestowed on all and room was allowed in the service for *the participation of all who were present.*[5] 'When you meet together,' says Paul, 'each of you hath a psalm, a teaching, a tongue, an interpretation.' (I Cor. 14:20) Every member was expected to contribute something of his own to the common worship. In most cases the contribution would be a modest one, a sentence or two of personal confession or adoration, or perhaps a mere 'Amen.' But there were those who were peculiarly gifted with the Spirit and who prophesied or engaged in ecstatic prayer. It is difficult to make out whether a special interval was allowed for those free devotions, or whether they accompanied the service throughout. Paul is himself anxious that they should be confined within limits."[6]

There is a connection between this spiritual freedom of genuine inspiration, and the power with which that obscure

[4] Acts 2.
[5] Italics mine.
[6] *The Nature of the Early Church*, pp. 79-80.

company swept across the Mediterranean world, balked neither by paganism nor persecution. The modern church has lost something, and needs to regain this kind of dynamic spiritual fellowship. For many church services are, frankly, so tame that no one coming into one of them is impelled by them to seek what these believers have, nor to feel that their faith holds the answer to his needs. It is probably wise to eliminate this spontaneous element from the regular services of the Church, but it should certainly be provided for at some other time. For it is clearly untrue to the Christian heritage, and unhappy in its effects, that our people should be so almost universally exposed to the *ideas* of their faith, and almost universally kept from *experiencing it together*. Such experience is often initiated in fellowship, and it is certainly fulfilled in fellowship. The rifted, separate particles of the Church, the individual believers, seldom have any least experience of what fellowship means. And inevitably this creates a reduced and stultified faith.

All true Christian fellowship can have but one objective: the building of the Kingdom on earth. No mere gathering for the sake of fellowship—no gathering simply to build up one another—we gather to pray, study, experience and work for just one thing, the coming of the Kingdom.

We must therefore understand what the Kingdom of God, or the Kingdom of Heaven, means. Jesus used these words continually. That Kingdom hung like a bright vision, gleaming ever in His mind's eye. It was apparently for Him that summation of good which all of us, not in our wildest, but in our soberest, dreams for the world pray and long and work to see achieved. Whatever He believed about its coming, the early Church certainly believed in its "eschatological" character, which simply means that it would never be wholly established except by the mighty, supernatural intervention of God; for man working on his own plane, even with the help of the grace of God, could not establish that Kingdom. The early Church knew very well the fundamental tension in life between God and goodness, and the Evil One and radical evil. A verse like I S. John 5: 19, "And we know that we are of God, and the whole world lieth in wickedness," is a realistic appraisal of the superhuman task of the Church. It was not until modern times that the Church in any large way abandoned this "eschatological" view of the Kingdom. It took modern liberalism to turn the Kingdom into a kind of infinite extension of social service, the product of that idealism which looks so much like Christianity but is actually so far from it, that compound of good will and sentimentality which is the inadequate ground-work of so much humanitarian kindness. Our dreams of a happier world where all is peace, and we can pursue our soft and selfish ways unmolested by care, or the assault of evil, forever, do not accord and are not consistent with Jesus' idea of the Kingdom. The belief that all this could come up and grow almost automatically till the world should be transformed by it is based on a view of human nature and of the world which is not the New Testament view. But it made very good soil in our time for the seeds of the greatest catastrophe history has seen to grow in; the two world wars sprang up while men were thinking in these terms, thus opening themselves to the onslaughts of that very radical evil they were denying by their rosy ideas of the world. The Kingdom of God is not inherent in history: it is to be born from without history, born by the supernatural action of God. It is only partially achieved in this world: beside the City of God stands the City of Man, where very different principles are at work. 'The world' is both the scene, and the enemy, of 'the Kingdom.' The demarcation between these is clearly shown in the Baptismal Service in the Book of Common Prayer where the question asked is, "Dost thou . . . renounce the devil and all his works, the vain pomp and glory of the world, with all covetous desires of the same, and the sinful desires of the flesh, so that thou wilt not follow, nor be led by them?" And the reply is, "I renounce them all; and, by God's help, will endeavour not to follow nor be led by them." We are to work constantly, ceaselessly towards the coming of the Kingdom. We are to fight evil wherever it is entrenched. The Kingdom appears partially fulfilled wherever men in their characters and in their relationships are obedient to the will of God.

This is the meaning and function of the Church. The Church is not the Kingdom—there are too many tares choking the wheat in the Church for us to be able to say that it is the Kingdom. In getting itself into the world, we all know how much of the world has gotten into the Church. But where the Church is faithful, where it is forgiven and empowered by the Spirit of God, there you have a corner, an outpost, an instance, of the Kingdom. Insofar as the Church was commissioned by Christ to be His arm in the world, the 'extension of the Incarnation,' the way by which people were to be brought into touch and kept in touch with Him, the Church is the Kingdom. The Word of God which comes to us through the Church, the Grace of God which comes to us through the Sacraments, the overarching Presence and Peace of God which we sometimes realize in corporate worship—these things are direct gifts of God, and are uncontaminated by men in their transmission. But in our practise as human members of the Church, in our obedience, in our fulfilment in life of all His commandments, we are woefully lacking, and fall far short of the Kingdom. It is ours to receive what comes to us from God through the Church, and it is ours to help purify whatever man's sins have done to the Church. It is the frankly supernatural side of the Church that has saved it from its own members all down through the centuries; it is this which makes it necessary for all men who want to be Christians to reckon with the Church and to be part of it, rather than going off to form their own little societies—where this has been done, in a few years these societies suffer from the same sins which made them dissatisfied with the Church. Christ left His Kingdom in the hands of the Church; insofar as it has failed of achievement, the sin lies mostly at the Church's door; and insofar as it has succeeded in its objective, the Church has been mostly responsible.

We cannot expect to see an instance of the Kingdom, even its beginnings, apart from a company of people where genuine 'relationship' has been achieved. Even a small parish may be too large to achieve such fellowship between all its members; it needs to be broken up into smaller companies where people can know one another, establish real relationships with one another, help each other in their various needs, keep each other checked up on whether they are living by Kingdom principles. The early church was sometimes called the 'ecclesia'—the called-out company; and sometimes the 'koinonia,' or the fellowship. We need the institutional Church, for religion cannot continue down the ages in a bodiless condition, any more than the spirit of men, (which is infinitely more important than the body) can be found in this world apart from the body. But a Church can be materialistic, just as a man can, and emphasize and develop those things which belong to its body, forgetting the things which belong to its soul. It is easier to be occupied with the institutional life of the church than with its spiritual power and mission. We easily slip down into it. That is why we must work double-time in these days to let the power of God come again into the Church, especially in the way of fellowship.

We are thinking about helping people. Now I want to

point out four ways in which fellowship, Christian fellowship, helps people:

1. Fellowship helps the individual to *find* faith. No one is free who is not free in relation to other people. Freedom is a spirit. Hostility, criticalness, fear, domination—these things in an atmosphere congeal men's souls, tie them in emotional knots, keep them from being themselves or giving what they can give. But friendliness, appreciation, faith, the desire to serve and help—these things in an atmosphere release men's souls, until their emotional knots, help them to be themselves and to give what they have to give. Berdyaev says, "Only a spiritual community liberates man."[7] You see, we do not take in faith until first the shell of self-consciousness, formality, unreality, fear, is broken, and we are open to it. I cannot enough emphasize the importance of fellowship in the finding of faith; the two things are married together, God has joined them together, and no man can put them asunder. Time was when men found faith in vast meetings where some great speaker preached evangelistic sermons: this does not appear characteristically to be such a time. There is always the necessity which we are emphasizing in this book, that one man help another man to find faith: that is an everlasting part of the way the Christian religion spreads. But there is a way in between these two which has not been sufficiently cultivated; the way of the small group, where a few people have found fellowship among themselves by caring, by candour, by mutual help, by prayer—and this is not an exclusive 'club,' the edges are open, others are welcomed, and through this rather impersonal personalness, the pores of men's souls are opened to a discovery of faith for themselves.

2. Fellowship helps people to *develop* faith. A letter lies before me from a person who has had a spiritual experi-

7 *Slavery and Freedom*, p. 108.

ence, and now needs to be developed and trained: it asks certain theological questions which would never have arisen if the first steps had not been taken, and some attempt made to impart the new-found faith to others. I am suggesting in my reply certain reading that will give a better foundation to faith. "Sometimes I'm up, sometimes I'm down," says the old Negro spiritual: and we all do go through periods of elation, and periods of depression, in our spiritual pilgrimage. We can help one another through them. One whose faith is strong and who is 'in power' can help another who is down to find out what has made him so: for there is always a reason. There is immense encouragement in hearing a man tell about how he came through a time of testing just like one you are going through yourself. When prayer is vague to you, and you hear a man talk about it as simply as if one were talking to a human Father, there is something for you to work on. There needs to be a certain amount of healthy collision where there is fellowship otherwise it becomes a sappy mutual admiration society. My experience is that when God comes into a man's life, He cures him of his sins; this victory is real, and may be permanent: but there easily develops a pride about this victory, a wilfulness in the way we use it, that constitutes another outcropping of real sin that needs to be dealt with. Often the old sin—say, of self-will or egotism—comes back under a different guise. Others often see this before we do, and can help us in its early stages, if we are willing to listen. We must "speak the truth in love," not in censoriousness, and not in self-will: but we must speak it. When we feel something about another person, and fail through fear or procrastination to say it, it cuts fellowship with him: and this failure is ours, not his.

3. Fellowship helps people to *multiply* faith. The average man, the average Christian, is so uninformed and so hesi-

tant about expressing his faith, that he never thinks of himself as able to help anyone else. Then he comes into a little company where everybody is helping everybody else. Some are mature and can help a lot; others are new and can help only a little. But they are out in the field of spiritual experimentation and action, not sitting on the side-lines as spiritual spectators and bench-warmers. We see there men whom we should not expect to see there. There is laughter in place of long faces. Men like ourselves are talking simply, honestly, unsentimentally. God is evidently doing something for them, making a difference. And they can speak of this intelligibly, in terms of laws and principles of faith that apply to everybody. We find there is a way to deal with an atheist, an alcoholic, a skeptic, a materialist, a pagan, an upright business man who feels no need for faith, and to help them. We learn how much example has to do with all this—yet what are the limitations of example. We see how genuine friendship can ripen into creative sharing of experience that leads on to real faith. We begin to take the first step, which may consist of bringing another man to this meeting next week. It begins to be natural for us to live out our faith at home, and at business, and to bring it into ordinary conversation in such a way that people are interested, not bored—so that they ask questions, rather than wanting to get away. Most people in the church never get to this place, though their ministers urge it upon them many times: and they do not get to it because they have not been brought into a small nucleus of people like themselves that have taken the plunge and 'got going.'

4. Fellowship helps people to *apply* faith. So much religion is in an 'ivory tower.' The wicked old world rolls on, and over to one side is a little pious nest of people who live to themselves; or if they make connection with the world at all, they often compromise to do it, and thus live in two unrelated compartments. But here is a smaller meeting

where for example, a C.I.O. leader begins speaking. He tells with a modest smile what he was able to do about a foreman the men all hated. He used to hate him, too. While he was on vacation painting his house one day he got to praying about him, and God said, "Love that foreman." Back at work the next week, he went into the boiler room; there was the foreman, sneezing his head off. "Got a cold?" he asked. "No," said the foreman, "hayfever." "Don't you think it would be better if the men did not use these air-hoses just before you come in here?" "Yes, it would," replied the foreman, "but they wouldn't coöperate." "I think they would if we asked them," answered the C.I.O. leader. It was all arranged, the airhoses played at a different time, so the foreman's hay-fever was better, so his disposition was better, so his handling of the men was better. He and the C.I.O. leader got so 'thick' that some other C.I.O. members complained their representative was becoming 'teacher's pet.' But the rest said, "Keep on, as long as you handle him this way, he keeps off our backs." So it all works in a boiler room, if somebody is really in touch with God. For all this goes back to the fact that, when a man was on vacation from work he was not on vacation from God; and when he would have liked merely to take sides, God told him to take responsibility instead. Nobody can listen to a simple, real story like that and then say, "Business is business— and you can't mix religion and business." The truth is that unless religion is mixed with business, business will go on getting rottener and rottener, and religion will go on getting rarer and rarer. The exchange of experience in fellowship shows people how faith can be applied every day.

Happily there is a steady increase in the number of these small companies that meet to find the better way. So many and so varied are they that some of us believe spiritual awakening may come in our time, not so much through transformed individuals alone, nor through great campaigns and big meetings, but through little companies of the Spirit. Some meet for breakfast or lunch, with half to three-quarters of an hour every week to talk, plan and pray. Some go apart for a week-end with leaders asked in to guide them. Some meet in offices, some in homes, some in churches. One group meets once a week for an hour of unbroken silence together, listening to God, and the men say it is the profoundest spiritual experience of their lives. Some study, some share experience, some spend much time in prayer, some work together on a community project that needs solving.

The Church should be, and in some instances is, taking the lead in the formation of such companies, generally led by lay-people. The Church needs to deepen its own life. One of our honest and scholarly clergy[8] declares that fellowship in the Church is "more hope than possession. We avoid deep religious fellowship," he goes on, "in order to avoid talking about the deepest things. Formal religion is an escape from the problems of our own living. This is due to fear. Our Church lacks a reality of Christian life. Every human being is important, and every little experience is important. Only in openness of Christian fellowship can anything happen: we have got to talk about *what we have experienced.*"

[8] The Rev. Cyril Richardson.

VII

Helping People to Keep Normal

ALL AROUND US today are people who are nearing the edge of nervous tension and breakdown, and day by day people are sliding over into a slough of anxiety, self-pity, fear, evasion of reality, from which it is going to be difficult for them to extricate themselves. If we are going to help people, we must know how to rescue those who have fallen over into this pit; but we must also know how to keep others from moving any closer to the edge of it.

Therefore in this chapter we are going to deal with the things that make for the maintenance of normality.

Normality means bodily and emotional health with its consequent sanity of outlook, from which we may lapse a little from time to time but to which we ordinarily return. Most people are born with this, but lose much of it on their way to mature growth. One of the things which genuine spiritual conversion brings about is a return to normality. So we shall be speaking of what keeps that normality insofar as it can be kept from the beginning, and what continues it once it has been regained, at least in some measure, through spiritual experience.

We begin at the simplest level with *health,*—physical health. A child is healthy when it gets enough food, sleep, air and exercise. As we grow older we tend to take liberties with one or more of these essentials. We eat hurriedly, too sparsely, too heavily, of the wrong things, or when our emotions are on tension and we should take very little.

[101]

Or we borrow on the strength that comes from sleep, and do not pay back. Most people need eight hours, and should have it. Most people will do better not to expend in a day more than they can make up in a night. Nobody can do this always, but it should be our aim always. Everybody should get into the air every day for at least half an hour of walk if possible; they should be friends with the sun and be at some time in the year marked with it. Of course our windows should be wide open at night. And we should have some exercise daily, the kind that makes us sweat if possible (Benjamin Franklin pointed out that this was the effective kind of exercise), that loses us in some absorbing work if possible (like carpentering, or gardening, or a well-loved game), and that makes us want to lay weary limbs in bed at night. As we get older, a short period of rest before or after lunch becomes desirable. These are very obvious things; but we may find ourselves trying to correct the breach of them by spiritual and psychological means, when the laws of health should have been followed all along. A high-strung, naturally energetic person needs to err on the side of giving himself extra rest: a sluggish and lazy person on the side of more exercise than he likes. We must find out what our nature needs, and provide it. A doctor's advice plus our own observation ought to help us. It is not normal to be thinking everlastingly about one's health; but neither is it normal to ignore it, for we or those who love us will pay for it later on if we do. There is a wise word from the late Dr. Alexander Whyte, of Edinburgh: "Squander your life, but be careful of your health."

Emotional health is closely allied to physical health: they interact on each other. A shock or anxiety can send up a healthy person's blood pressure or send their metabolism up or down beyond the normal: and the control of emotion is one of the greatest problems of our time. For some years education despised emotion, and treated it like a step-child in the family of human qualities. Thus we have seen a generation of mental adults many of whom were emotional infants. Emotion is the driving-power of life: it cannot be suppressed, it must come out some way. The problem is to find the right places for our emotions to feed. We can feed them with hate, and they will corrode the whole mechanism. We can feed them with love, and they will tone up the whole mechanism. Real anger can prevent sleep for hours, it can cause food to be undigested, it can cause violent head-aches. A great human love, or passionate devotion to a worthy cause, can keep our emotions supplied with almost unlimited fresh energy, and so make for good physical health as well. Strong emotions, well under control, able to be consciously put at the service of adequate objectives, not only make prodigious amounts of work possible but make them seem easy. Most of us can learn to control our emotions outwardly, so that we do not fly into a rage when something provokes us, or go into a depression when a great disappointment comes to us. The deeper problem, however, is to let the control go down into the subconscious, so that there is no more disturbance there than on the surface. This takes much training, and I think it takes considerable help from outside ourselves.

There is something in man that is different from his body, and from his emotions; and that is his spirit. He needs health of body, health of emotions, and *health of spirit*. Now health of spirit, as I see it, is faith. On the plane of daily living, it is courage and confidence: on the inner plane, it is trust and dependence on God. Real faith seems almost inseparable from the full current of life itself. Faith believes that if it should be done, it can be done. Faith believes in its own visions and desires and dreams. Faith has prayed about these things, talked them over with God, asked God to remove them if they are not in accordance with His plans, and to bless them if they are. Faith feels the universe at its back. It is moving with the universe, not bucking against it. It believes every problem has a solution, every question has an answer,—else it would not be there. To faith these things are not obstructions and personal attacks on the part of fate; they are like handicaps in a race that is meant to be run—and won. Faith is not blind to evil, nor unacquainted with fear: but it is, as someone said, "fear that has said its prayers." At bottom and when all is said and done, the kind of faith we are talking about is predicated on belief in a personal God, Who knows us, loves us, tests us sometimes, even chastises us, but loves us through everything and does everything for our good and everybody's good. That is why St. Paul can say, "All things work together for good to them that love God." "*All* things," mind you, not some things. "Work *together,*" not separately. "For *good,*" not always for pleasure or peace of mind or the satisfaction of the ego. "To *them that love God,*" not just to everybody, but to the people with faith. Everybody longs for that kind of faith that binds life into a unity, that lifts suffering up into significance, that gives continuous zest to the very experience of being alive.

Now where shall we find these three great ingredients of normality?

There is nothing else that can take the place of a *stable, happy, secure home*. For these things to be normal for a child, they should surround him from the first. If he grows up in them, and they compass him about in his formative years, he can stand a good deal that is far removed from them in his later years. Parents that love their children, that are healthy in body, emotionally sound, and spiritually believing people, can give something to their children that nothing else can give, and that nothing else can take away. Parents like this create an orderly home life, and that helps children to develop orderliness in their inner lives. The most stable people that I see are people whose childhood was filled with affection, quiet and orderly. Regularity in family life— as to meals, hours, responsibilities—yet with that flexibility in the parents that allows for rightful exceptions—is part of a child's security now and training for the future. Parents who keep their word and promises, who do not buy beyond their income, who face cheerfully whatever arises, are building a priceless quality into their children. A dining-room table which is a kind of family melting pot, where everybody gives himself or herself to the rest of the family, where there is plenty of chance for uninhibited talk, much laughter, consideration for others, and general give-and-take, is a great training for life in a democracy. When cheerfulness and gayety are found at home, children will want to be at home and to bring their friends home with them.

As I write, I am thinking how far some homes I know are from this idea. Sometimes I see children living, first with one, then another, of divorced parents, sometimes in harum-scarum apartments with no system, no regular hours for meals, no fixed, steady points in their lives; and I know what emotional tensions are being created in these children. Sometimes I see parents so preoccupied, through work or worry or general indiscipline, that they never have time to give themselves in leisure, in play, in serious talk, to their children; and I know that something irreparable is being lost. Besides these things that could be corrected, there are the situations made difficult by inescapable facts—one parent working at very irregular hours, or emotionally a little unstable, lack or loss of love between them, one plagued with poor health, another with sick relatives that claim much time, and perhaps little money or room. What then? What chance for healthy, happy, believing children with so many of the cards stacked against them?

How You Can Help Other People

Well, it all depends on how much of the right spirit the parents have. I'd like to take you to a simple apartment, where an educated father and mother are bringing up three children. The father is creative with his hands, yet is forced to 'push a pen.' The mother is by nature an artist, loves space and quiet and seclusion, and must cook, wash, keep house for the five of them. It is one of the soundest homes I know. You feel it the moment you cross the threshold. The parents are real parents, the children are real children. None of the fear of parents on the part of browbeaten children; and none of the very common fear of children on the part of parents who will do almost anything to hold their children's affection. There is welcome, courtesy, manners, a sense of something stable, permanent and secure,—almost a sense of wealth amid this simplicity. Whence come these things? Not from easy temperaments, for they are strong and diverse. They come from faith. That family believes in God. They are in church on Sunday. They believe in God seven days a week. No wonder the children are healthy and well. I'll wager that when the strains come to them in five, ten, twenty-five years, they will meet them in the kind of strength that is being built into them now through stability, responsibility, coöperation, and faith. A real family, with God in the middle of it—there is one of the great sources of normality in our troubled time.

Public worship which the family attends together is another source of health and normality in people. Here Sunday after Sunday the family meets as a family, but in a new aspect: they are made part of a very large family in the world, the family of God. They are conscious that all over the world others are meeting like this. They say prayers that others are saying, they listen to sermons that emphasize the whole world-wide family of God. They are lifted out of a narrow family life into a wide one. They worship together, father and mother bowing before the same God as the children; so that a strong feeling of equality before God is present. The security which they feel because father and mother are dependable people is lifted up to a cosmic level, and they feel the undergirding power of believing in a God of love. Here they will meet people of all kinds, of different backgrounds; and if the church is really Christian, they will see a working democracy, for all will be welcome, all will be accepted, all will take responsibility. The service may be a little "over their heads" while they are little: no matter—let them keep coming, and bit by bit they will grasp more of it. You should teach the same truths to them at home, but these will be deepened as children hear them reiterated again and again, in different ways, in church. No child for whom church-going is only occasional will have this benefit. One of the great values of a liturgy is that one is constantly taking in truth while he is giving out worship; the words he uses to express his devotion are words which frame for him careful religious thought. There is no way of estimating the rich effect upon us of these early exposures to the Church in the company of our families. This can hardly help being a real high point of the week. And its unconscious effect upon families is literally incalculable. The more fixed is attendance at church, the more fixed the child's convictions that faith comes first in life. Dr. Henry C. Link has said some startling things of the permanent effect for good upon the personalities of children who attend church and Sunday-School.

And then there is the great importance of public worship for those who have wandered out into a spiritual no-man's-land, and found it arid. Thousands have done it under the impetus of modern education. Then they marry, and children begin coming along. Life lays its weights upon us, and sometimes they are too heavy for us to bear alone. A

woman came in seeking spiritual help. She was very modern, a college graduate, a writer, and her husband overseas.
She had been through a nervous break-down and been
greatly helped by a psychiatrist. "But," she said, "I don't
want to get into that frame of mind again, so I have begun
coming to church." She and her children have been bap-
tized, and come with great regularity, though there was
never any formal religion in her life before. She is finding the steadying-power of worship in her life and the life
of her children. The Church is helping to conserve the
work that had to be done by a psychiatrist. That work
might never have had to be done if she had had the
Church earlier, and known the security in her life of a
working, practising faith.

Another great element in building soundness and
normality into people is *private worship*. Primarily this
means the study of the Bible, and prayer. These two together do certain things for us. They re-align us with the
will of God in which we believe but which we often lose
hold of in the constant exposures of busy life, and re-estab-
lish its force in our hearts. They bring the reality of forgiveness to us, after we have failed to live up to the high
resolves we made in prayer before, or have disobeyed God.
They lift us above a self-centered depression that may have
come from fatigue, from a quarrel, from boredom, from
failure, by centering our emotions again in God and His
power instead of our own weaknesses. They reaffirm for
us the Reality of God, and His governance and sovereignty
in His world, when tragedy has come upon us or our
friends and brought sorrow close to home. They put actual
strength into us in the place of human weakness. They con-
fer the illumination of God upon problems and questions
and choices where human judgment lacks direction and
conviction. They hold us down from undue elation, and up
from undue depression, and on the even keel of the will of

God. Each day they remind us that God is the everlasting
background of our lives, and renew the contact of His
Spirit with ours. All of this is bound to be a stabilizing,
normalizing influence. How many times has one seen a
person kept and held through great crisis by the living
power of God, and another held away from slipping over
into a collapse of nerves, and another even from the abyss
of insanity itself! We cannot say too often that life lived
in our own strength is simply too much for us. The alter-
nation of effort and relaxation, which is the essence of
religious practise, cannot be enjoyed: if everything rests
upon us, then we must live by our own effort. One may
manage this for a time; but there comes a day when a special strain is added to the usual, and we snap. But cultivate
these inner resources, cultivate them over the long, quiet
places in life, so that a reserve is established: and when the
crisis is there you will draw on those reserves just as you
can draw on reserves in a bank account. People wonder
where the courage and resourcefulness and indomitable
hope of China's Generalissimo Chiang Kai Shek comes
from: a good deal of it probably comes from his systematic
personal devotional life. There is something more, something unplumbed, inexhaustible, about the inner resources
of a man who keeps in touch with God through prayer and
the Bible.

And there is also a great strength where *parents and
children share in family devotions* at home. In addition to
what each one does privately, the whole family ought to
meet together for prayer, Bible reading, meditation, worship, perhaps hymns, some time in the day. More informal
than public worship, yet more social than merely private
devotion, the family reaffirms its own faith and redis-
covers its basic security together once a day. If this is
rushed, unreal, dogmatic in tone, or all carried on by parents, it will fail to touch the children. If children partici-

pate, by their own prayers, reading, questions, problems to be talked about, if there is variety of procedure and reality in what the adults do, this will keep freshness and interest for the children. If interest flags as children grow older, it may be well to let them stop it for a time, and return to it on a new basis later on. But it is a good thing for a family to lose self-consciousness enough to hear each other pray aloud, read the Bible, and talk naturally of the bearing of faith on daily problems. This must never be used as a whip-handle by which anyone seeks to control anyone else: let it be an honest search on the part of all to have God control everybody.

All these "means of grace" are meant to help us more and more to know and do the will of God. Through them, God makes His will known to us. In their light we see a certain course as selfish, short-sighted, foolish, inadequate, wrong; and another as unselfish, wise, right and guided. Most of us do not linger long enough in God's Presence to find His will. We need often to be quiet, silent, open, waiting for His thoughts, His feelings, His direction, to become ours. Let us often *enjoy* God, seeking nothing but himself. Prayer is not intended to change the will of God, but to discover it. The bombardment of God by human wilfulness is not Christian prayer. Prayer is mutual exchange, our needs and desires ascending to Him, His grace and His will descending to us. Some while ago I talked with a college professor who was having difficulty at home. I asked him if he and his wife ever prayed. "Of course we do—we are Christian people," he said. "What do you do when you pray?" I asked. And he said, "I just keep telling God over and over what I want." I said, "Did it ever occur to you that some day God might say to you, 'Which of us *is* God anyway: are you telling Me, or am I telling you?'" It was a new thought to him that prayer was not a way to get your own will, but a way to find the will of

God. The more we pray to know Him, to find His will, to be obedient to it, the more we shall know.

Another factor in creating and maintaining normality is the *right vocation*. This is the will of God as applied to one's life work. Henry Drummond said that God has a will for career as well as for character. Most of us leave a 'call' to ministers or missionaries, and ourselves go and do what we like or what seems sensible. But it is here that we begin to muss the plans of God: He has a will, a plan, a place for everybody, and no one else can take or fill that place. Vocation arises from a combination of three factors:

1. The objective need of the world.
2. Our personal talents and capacities.
3. The revealed will of God for us.

A gifted and brilliant fellow who could write light opera with genius gave his life to Christ, and soon the question of vocation faced him: he decided to go into full-time Christian work because, as he said with a twinkle, "the world needs another Phillips Brooks more than it needs another Victor Herbert." Most of us do not sufficiently consider the objective need. But then we must honestly look at our own talents. There are gifts and capacities, even more are there curiosities, 'pulls,' concerning one or another kind of work; and these must be considered, for they may have been put within us by God to help us discover what He wants of us. Let us come with all the facts we can find, and lay our lives humbly before Him asking Him to show us what He wants us to do. Slowly the weight of conviction falls one way or the other, and we feel drawn to choose a profession, a business, an art. Marriage is part of vocation, and much unhappiness arises from self-will about the person we are going to marry. If we let God decide it, if God is from the first a Third Party to an engagement or a marriage, it will be contracted upon a sound and secure and lasting basis. Far too many people today are pushed into jobs by what appears to be necessity, who ought to be pushed only by conviction that a given course is the will of God. There is possibly no one thing that gives so much inner strength to a person as believing that they are in the place where God intends them to be. There need be nothing of conceit or complacency about this: if God is God, then He has a will for every detail of His universe, for every life He has created. We find that will when we seek it in honesty and surrender. "If any man willeth do his will he shall know. . . ."[1]

If we are to help people to become or to remain normal, we must help them to find an outlet for their aggressive instincts. In the raw, these are destructive; and if they do not have the proper objectives, they will let themselves out against the wrong ones. Whether they come from our remote and savage ancestors, or from the fear of non-recognition, obscurity or extinction on the part of our own ego, we are all possessed of deep instincts of pugnacity. Fear may underlie much of this. What can be done with this raw energy? Dr. Karl Menninger has written a valuable book on this theme, called *Love Against Hate*. In it he says, "Evil itself rather than persons felt to be foes becomes the object of the destructiveness, and the individual is then on the threshold of complete maturity. . . . All aggressive energy except that small quantity necessary for self-defense against real dangers is turned into useful channels and employed in the services of living and loving. Aggression, destructive energy, is thus effectively denatured, and by a shift in object and modality it becomes constructive. This latter process constitutes *sublimation,* as I view it."[2] He shows how the savagery and destructiveness of child-

[1] St. John 7:17.
[2] *Op. cit.,* pp. 128-9.

hood may be turned into useful fields, as in the case of a child who had been sent to a correctional school because of his compulsion to burn down his father's garage, and became the chief of the fire prevention program! At first aggression is directed at what stands in its own path. Growing maturity turns the aggression against what stands in the path of humanity, human society. We begin to hate, not that evil which conflicts with our own will (a very doubtful, immature conception of evil), but that which conflicts with the onward progress of men generally. The problem of vocation, and the problem of satisfactorily sublimating one's own aggressive instincts, is the problem of finding some one area into which one can pour one's pugnacity against some form of evil. A teacher's life is, if you like, a long battle against ignorance, a doctor's against sickness, a scientist's against stubborn nature, a minister's against unhappiness and evil. Let us recognize the nobility of a 'call' to take up some one profession or work in life; but let us not fail to draw to our aid these deep, instinctual energies which put emotional content into our work, and keep us persistent and enthusiastic in it. Nothing can better drain away the petty out-croppings of temper, irritation and moods (which can do so much not only to sap our own energies, but also to spoil the lives of those about us) than to use up all our pugnacious energies in a real fight against the real enemy on the front where we have chosen to fight.

Clearly the *making of friends* is one of the most important elements in normality. Going through life and meeting many people, we instinctively know that here is one, or there is one, that is meant to be more than 'ships that pass in the night.' Long-range friendships are a good sign of normality, and short-range ones of its opposite. In real friendship, we give our best. And if we have faith, that faith is the best thing we have; we shall therefore want it to become part of every friendship if possible. The highest

form of friendship is fellowship in Christ: this lifts and
transforms ordinary human relations into something not
merely congenial or selfishly pleasant, but constructive and
creative. We do not merely accept one another as we are,
but help one another to grow and to become spiritually effective. How many of us would have been spared getting
into ruts, idiosyncrasies, moods, temptations, real evil
ways, neuroticism, if we had had people to whom we could
go and talk things out and get set straight! How much
less work would there be for doctors and psychiatrists if
all of us took responsibility for a few people, prayed for
them, saw them personally, met with them in a small company once a week! How many would be kept from loneliness, fear, bitter resentment towards life, if they were
part of such a spiritual fellowship! Why not start one? If
you are going to build a fire, you need three things: sticks,
fire and a draught. You can't make a fire with one log: it
takes several. One human heart, alight for Christ, humble,
laughing, giving—that is the fire. And the wind that blows
through the whole to make it burn is the Holy Spirit. Two
companies there are, which are the antitheses of each
other: little brotherhoods of love and fire like this, and
large aggregations of tragic people in mental institutions.
Perhaps we must choose which company we shall have;
for without more faith and more fellowship, the mounting
mental sickness of today will become such a burden upon
normal people as we can hardly bear.

Normality certainly involves time and place for *play*.
The typical neurotic never plays—he slaves at his work,
often beyond normal hours, and always finds some excuse
why he cannot enjoy himself. The truth is, he has lost the
capacity for enjoyment, if he ever had it; and his way back
to normality must sometimes pass the place of absorbed
enjoyment in something which he does principally because
he enjoys it. It may be a pleasure that has a useful side, like

carpentering, fishing, gardening; but this is in a sense incidental. The more interests we have in which we can lose ourselves, the better adjusted we are likely to be: psychologists know that people with hobbies are better adjusted than those without them. Some pleasures we shall take with others, some by ourselves. If our work confines us, we shall seek companionship in pleasure: if our work throws us much with people, we shall need times of play alone. We sometimes seek for medical or psychological help for states of mind we could cure ourselves if we knew how to lose ourselves in play. I remember one winter when various factors had kept me for many weeks from a 'day off:' my nerves were tired and tense, it took two hours to do an hour's work. I got off to the country, found a clean piece of pine board, a saw and a hammer, and went to making some gadget for the house. I lost myself completely in it; and within an hour I began feeling the health creeping up my arms from my fingers. That night I slept soundly and next day was entirely rested. We all need a period of 'time out' for play and rest in every day, in every week, and in every year. Incidentally I commend to ministers taking Saturdays off, instead of Mondays: this not only refreshes us for Sunday, and gives us plus energy and keeps us from looking tired and so taking it out of our people; but it is better to think of something we might say tomorrow than to think of something we wish we had said yesterday! Give yourself a chance to play, and get the people you want to help to do it also. Not just 'spectator' play, like going to the movies or a baseball game, but something they do with other people or make with their own hands.

We must take care also for *what we accept into our thinking*. There is a strange contrast between society's care in creating pure-food laws so strict that water, ice cream, food, in almost any small public place, are quite safe, and its lack of concern about taking into the mind fear, negative suggestion, deteriorating thought, resentment. These things are forms of poison, as much as wellwater with typhoid germs in it; yet we will take almost anything into the mind which is temporarily agreeable. It looks to me as if the mind were a kind of vacuum that is constantly asking to be filled; if we have not positive, creative material to pack into it, then it will fill up with negative and destructive material. Here again, there is one inexhaustible fountain of hope, peace and cheerfulness: and it is faith. The ideas of faith are cosmic in magnitude. The plans of faith do not stop short of a 'new heaven and a new earth.' The energy of faith is like the undiminished energy of radium. Of course people are normal and well, far beyond the usual, when faith is their growing possession. It will help us in this connection to store our minds with the best reading we can do in the field of faith. Such books as *The Return to Religion,* by Henry C. Link; *In Search of Maturity,* by Fritz Kunkel; *A Testament of Devotion,* by Thomas R. Kelly; *Abundant Living,* by E. Stanley Jones; and most of the writings of William Temple, late Archbishop of Canterbury, and of C. S. Lewis, will prove informing and inspiriting.

To sum up, then: whether we want to keep the normality we have, or to restore that which we have lost, it will help us to take care of our health, bodily and emotional; to cultivate faith; to give time to building sound homes with God at the center of them; to go to church as families; to practise prayer and the study of the Bible; to cultivate corporate family worship; to seek the will of God, for our vocation and for daily details; to find the right outlet for our aggressive instincts, to make friends with whom we have the greatest possible degree of fellowship in spiritual things; to play; and to feed our minds on positive suggestions and on Christian truth. Most of this seems to concern direct religion; it does—the upbuilding of our faith, in our hearts, our homes and our churches, is the surest way to have enough of it with which to withstand, to penetrate, and to change the world about us. Let us keep such healthiness of outlook as we retain; and let us be thankful that the coming of God into any human life that has missed the way means the return to normality.

VIII

Helping the Physically Sick[1]

SCIENCE RECOGNIZES over two hundred diseases; and all of us are at some time brought into touch with sickness. Our sympathies are immediately aroused, but we often feel too inexperienced to do more than say a word of passing cheer or encouragement. People who are ordinarily well are apt to feel that they have not been "initiated" into the experience of serious illness, and therefore should not attempt to help those who are undergoing it. It is a curious fact that to see someone we know and love in a hospital bed, or bandaged up after an accident, sometimes puts up a strange little psychological barrier between them and us, and makes them seem a little remote from us, just at the very moment when they may need us more than ever. We should prepare ourselves for this reaction beforehand, and counteract it as much as possible.

There are two things which we all desire for sick people (1) that they may be cured if this is possible, and (2) that they find all the strength available with which to meet the sickness, and derive any benefit from it which can be found. There is a mystery about human sickness and pain, as there is a mystery about all the evil in the world. Pain can have its uses, and we have seen people

[1] I gratefully acknowledge the immense help I have received, not only in writing this chapter, but in all my dealings with sick people, from the book, *The Art of Ministering to the Sick,* by Richard C. Cabot and Russell L. Dicks. It remains the classic in this field.

meet it with a victory that constitutes a genuine triumph over the ills of the body, a noble assertion that the spirit can dominate the flesh. This line of argument follows that of William Temple, when he says that evil, when overcome, is justified. Jesus Christ, asked by His disciples whether it was a blind man himself, or his parents, who sinned and caused his blindness, said, "Neither hath this man sinned, nor his parents: but that the works of God should be made manifest in him."[2] Thereupon He healed him. We must always take this practical attitude towards sickness, not so much theorizing about it, as seeing what can be done to relieve it, and let God come in through it.

Some sickness arises through the breaking of laws—the laws of health or moral laws. When people put in too many hours of work and not enough of sleep, when they do not take enough exercise nor watch their diet with enough care, or when worry is added to a schedule already filled with as much work as can be put through, sickness is likely to result. The conflict caused by too great a discrepancy between one's convictions and one's practise is a fruitful source of poor health. A man gave his chief a promise that if he were appointed to a certain office, he would fall in with his chief's policy: after the appointment, he welched on his promise and opposed him; maybe this accounts for the nervous manner, the ashy skin, the obvious tensions in his life. A farmer left a place where he stole chicken-feed: he has not been well since he left nor been able to work. Such resulting sickness can be called a 'punishment' if you like; most people would prefer to call it the outworking of a law. We all know that we never do and never can break laws: we ignore or disobey them, and they break us.

There is a materialistic view of sickness which attributes it all to bodily factors, and treats it with medicine or the

[2] St. John 9: 3.

knife. And there is an airy view of sickness that attributes it all to mental factors, believing that it comes from wrong thinking and emotional states of mind. The truth may lie somewhere in the middle. One hears of the rise of a new 'school' of medicine called "psychosomatic" medicine—'psychos' meaning mind in Greek, and 'soma' meaning body. One would hardly think it necessary to call such a piece of ancient and elementary common-sense a new 'school.' For obviously there are physical and mental factors in all disease, which inter penetrate each other inextricably: both must be reckoned with, and both must be helped. People who want attention but cannot get it in any other way will sometimes make themselves sick through their emotions. Emotional factors can be so great that they cause almost every symptom of genuine disease. Depending on the bank-account, this can be kept up indefinitely. We have all known people who were sick because they had nothing else to do, no other way of being important, no other method of making people pay attention to them.

In serious and genuine illness, the emotions play an enormous part. Dr. Richard C. Cabot and the Rev. Russell L. Dicks says[3] that "A man carries into his illness the interests, affections, emotions, conflicts that have governed him hitherto. They raise his blood-pressure, they upset the movements of his heart, his stomach, and his bowels. They pervert the chemistry of his digestion and of his metabolism. The medical profession sees these connections better today than twenty years ago." For this reason anyone who can help sick persons to control their emotions, or can instil positive emotions into them instead of negative, will be of some assistance in their cure.

These are some of the common emotions of sick people. First, *fear*—fear of going to the hospital of which many people have an emotional dread, disliking such smells as

[3] *The Art of Ministering to the Sick,* p. 7.

ether or disinfectant as some people dislike the smells of a ship,—fear of an operation, of taking ether, of having a weak heart that cannot stand it, of somebody making a mistake—fear of dying, not always of what lies on the other side of death but of meeting it with cringing instead of courage, of the actual physical experience of dissolution, —fear of not having enough money to handle the hospital expense, or a long convalescence, or having enough health to carry on one's work afterwards. One hears pretty awful sounds sometimes in hospitals, and sees pretty terrible sights: the emotions store these things up in memory, and in the long watches of the night when sleep is a stranger these pictures come alive again with a plaguing power. Second, *loneliness.* There are long hours by day and night: a patient may be too sick to read or listen to the radio—too sick to see many callers or stand a long visit. One can feel very forsaken in a ward or in a private room, and magnify the absence of those whose duties may not permit them to come more often. Third, *boredom.* A well person is stricken down, none of his ordinary occupations or pastimes are possible for him, just hours of waiting, living more reduced to his own thoughts than ever just at a time when he needs some simple stimuli towards new thoughts, or some little diversion to get his mind off himself. It is in these long, lonely, bored hours that negative emotions may get a hold and do their greatest damage. Fourth, *resentment.* One feels neglected by the family and friends, one begins thinking the patient across in the other bed is getting more attention from the nurses, or some old wound of pride or hurt feelings opens again and provides a kind of bitter root to chew on through tiresome hours. Some time notice what sixty seconds of genuine hate or resentment can do to twist your own stomach: and then realize what this can do to retard the convalescence of a patient. Fifth, *self-pity.* Sometimes one sees a person back in hospital three, four, five times, with painful, tedious tests to be made, with days or weeks of suffering to be borne; and it is a struggle for them to keep from feeling that life is against them, that they have been unfairly singled out for all this pain and trouble.

Most patients want to be and to appear good sports. Some of them will complain and find fault with doctors, nurses and hospital. But most of them do their best to co-operate and make the best of things. Such people as these, however, need especially to be able to talk out with some-one their emotional troubles. They may be a little ashamed to do this, and apologize for it; but a wise counsellor or friend will draw them out, not let them think it is "foolish" to feel this way, or to want to talk about it, and let them say everything that is on their minds, without attempting to suggest an answer until they have said all that they are thinking. Often there lingers one thing which they are afraid or ashamed to say, e.g. that they are afraid of dying, or they really want to die, or have thought about suicide; or some old wrong has come to mind again and they want to be sure of forgiveness by God and the person they hurt. We must not pooh-pooh these things, nor leave them hanging. Out in the open, such a thing as considering suicide is probably over and done. But the offer to write a note for them to someone whose forgiveness they want may bring great emotional relief; while the visit of a minister may be desirable in the case of one who feels unforgiven by God.

It is always important that we work with and not against the doctor. After all, he is in charge of the case; his professional reputation is at stake, and he knows the medical factors. We should defer to him in all matters that concern the medical side of the case, as long as he is in charge of it: we should do well not to enter into a dispute about whether another doctor should be brought in—that is for the patient and the family to decide. None of us should set up as amateur doctors or psychiatrists, and doctors are not impressed by laymen who know a lot of medical terms: technical knowledge belongs rather to them, and they like to have a few obscure terms in which to talk among themselves and with which to impress patients and visitors, as clergy like to trot out a few theological terms a little over the layman's head. Doctors will naturally be sensitive about whether what we say backs up the course they are taking; we do well to consult the nurse and ask if there is any special advice we should have before going in. Doctors are interested in what they can do by medicine to cure this sick person. The philosophy of it does not interest them at the moment. They will judge of any visitor by the results of his call, welcoming or rejecting his assistance according to what he produces. If the patient is better after his call, and next day, the doctor will be glad to have him come back: if he stays too long, tires or excites the patient, he will not be welcome again. Short visits are generally best. The fact that ministers have free access to patients in hospitals at all hours make it tremendously important that they should work in the fullest collaboration with the doctor.

We come now into the sick-room. We give off a first impression, almost without knowing it. One whom perhaps we last saw in evening clothes is dressed in a hospital night-shirt, seldom becoming to anyone. The hair is rumpled, perhaps, the skin yellow, the eyes weary, maybe sunken. We must not appear startled, nor change our expression. Cheerfulness, confidence, quietness—those are the things a sick person hopes for in a visitor. If they are very sick, we shall take them gently by the hand remembering that there seems to be a kind of electricity that carries a wave of health over from a well to a sick person—they borrow our strength and feed on it. We shall speak quietly and clearly and simply, not taxing them with long sentences, or questions that have to be answered, or apolo-

gies that we did not come sooner. We have but a few
minutes with them, and we want to give off encouragement, strength, sympathy, power. "I am very sick and
weak," they may say. And we may reply, "Yes, I know:
it's no fun to be very weak. But the Bible says, 'When I
am weak, then am I strong,' because those are the times
when we rest back on God's strength because we have
none of our own. Just rest on God with your feelings as
your body is resting on this bed right now. 'Underneath
are the everlasting arms.' " I said that to a woman very
sick with heart-trouble, and dying: even in the confusion of
later delirium, that seemed to stick—she would ask the
nurse, "What was it he said?" And the nurse would repeat
it as nearly as she could remember. She had abundant and
beautiful faith—that woman—but she was too weak to
voice it for her own comfort, and needed someone to put
it in a simple way. "Rest on God with your emotions as
your body is resting on this bed"—somehow that stayed
with her.

Even when they are not terribly weak or sick, we shall
still want to step down the tempo of our life to theirs. Our
movements will be quiet and slow, not quick and jerky.
We shall not bump against the bed, nor shake it, nor sit on
it. If we sit down, we shall move the chair so that they
may look at us without uncomfortably turning their heads
or stand if their heads cannot be raised. They may want to
hear of what we have been doing: let us try to interest
them without exciting them. A funny story may help, or an
amusing experience, or one where someone has found a
greater faith. Sickness is a sobering experience, and
people who are ill want us to be real with them. We may
watch for some cue as to what they want to hear, or what
is on their minds. If the pain is bad, they may welcome
prayer, during which we may lay our hands quietly on
their foreheads—there is something in *touch,* or Christ

would not have put His hands upon people when He healed them. We shall not get on to controversial points, or such as are calculated to arouse their emotions; we should get into no discussion or arguments with them—if something you say produces a strong reaction, back out and start another subject. If faith has put into our lives a plus of energy (and it should), we must give off just enough of this energy to strengthen them, not enough to tire them. With a vigorous woman that had plenty of faith in God, I went to call on another woman in a hospital who was more sick with discouragement and hope deferred than she was with physical illness, though she was physically ill, too. We stayed but a short time; but she told her friend later that our visit "made her envious of good health of body and mind," and she decided then and there to get well if she could. She got much better and found a real faith, though the body was never wholly restored.

We can help sick people very much by telling them when they may expect us again, and then not failing them in that appointment; it gives them something to look forward to. As we leave, the condition of the patient and their need, the state of their faith or of our relation to them, may determine whether they want us to say a prayer. It should not be our unreadiness or our self-consciousness that determines it. Every clergyman knows what it is to kneel down beside a ward-bed, and pray with a sick person, no matter how many are talking, or looking on or whatever else is happening. Prayer should include all the people about the patient. It should be short, simple, out of our hearts, related to the person's need, honest, expecting real help, spoken in a voice of calmness and assurance.

Sometimes a patient will say, "Am I coming out of this?" And if we do not know the probable outcome, we can say, "Certainly your own faith is going to help you"; and if the doctor thinks the prospect not hopeful, we may not feel we should answer the question, but simply say, "Have you asked the doctor about this?" if they have been told they are probably not going to get well, wait to see if they want to talk about it; if so we shall talk simply and clearly about immortality and the way faith in Christ is the foundation of believing in it, giving them the assurance that *we* think all is well, not according to whether we stay here or go beyond, but because God is our Father. We shall want to leave them some word, some verse from Scripture, something to remember our visit by and to turn over in their minds after we have gone—something big and simple and positive and easy to grasp: "The Lord is my shepherd," "Thou shalt keep him in perfect peace whose mind is stayed on thee," "Commit thy way unto Him, and He shall bring it to pass."

In the case of those who appear to be dying, we must be careful what we say or allow to be said around them: sometimes all senses are numb but that of hearing. To have the conversation turn to trivialities, or to discouraging words about them, must be a very great shock to those who can give no sign of understanding. Over a woman who was dying, the doctor leaned and said to her family, "I am afraid this little lady is going down." The spunky little lady was not so sick as he thought, and said with her eyes still closed, "I am not going anywhere just yet; and when I go, I'm going *up!*" Those who are dying and still afraid to die will best be helped, I think, not by arguments for the belief in immortality, but rather by catching our own faith in it and beginning to trust God for everything, including the future. "I go to prepare a place for you," "Because I live, ye shall live also" these are the kind of verses to use. And when the life has been careless or worse, let us urge a simple prayer for forgiveness, and a trust in the promise, "Shall not the judge of all the earth do right?" We shall want to be as much as possible with those who are dying: we cannot know what comfort it is just to know there is someone there who cares for them. And there is another reason. Dr. Alfred Worcester of Harvard told me once that he sought to be present at the death of every person whom he cared for, because sometimes the signs of the opening of the other world were so convincing, as when a patient rises up in bed with eyes open in surprised delight, and speaks to someone who has gone before him into the world to come: he felt there was real evidence sometimes of the reality of immortality in the hour when a soul slips away from the body.

What of our ministry to the old, the shut-in, the chronic invalids? Their best help, beside adequate physical care, will be a daily routine to which they hold faithfully: to go from hour to hour, knowing what the next hour will contain, makes the day go faster. Better yet if they can find a real job to do in their confined life. A very active person, very wealthy and much interested in foreign missions, found herself confined and dying with cancer: I went to see her one day, and her spirit was as eager as ever, and she said, "You know, Mr. Shoemaker, I am having a wonderful experience. For the first time in my life, I have time enough to pray for all the people I want to pray for, as long as I like!" Intercession became her daily occupation.

Dr. Richard Cabot tells of a French Canadian sewing-woman who came to the Massachusetts General Hospital, had a leg amputated, and settled down for convalescence in the surgical ward. Soon a great improvement was noted in the morale of the whole ward. She had all the rest of the patients sewing with her, filled with enthusiasm for making the most of their lives. She got out, started a business of her own employing cripples like herself. She had to have the other leg amputated; but has kept on, first with her own business, then in a Catholic home, supervising sewing cripples. She writes, "My intention is the sanctification of incurables. We will gather up their pain and sufferings and present them to God. He will teach us to suffer in union with Him. I wish the sick were organized into one great body of prayful sufferers. . . . Sometimes I wonder if anyone is happier than I am. . . ." Dr. Cabot says part of her success comes because "she is constantly overflowing with happiness, affection, and with gratitude to God and to man."[4] Nothing will do more for those who suffer chronic pain, or are shut-in, or face long illnesses, than to find a useful vocation that can be pursued within the limits which their illness sets; and the cultivation of a spirit and habit of gratitude.

What of spiritual healing? The New Testament is full of it: you find it on almost every page of the Gospels. And down through the Christian centuries there has always been some spiritual healing, though apparently not in quite the proportion found in the early Church. It is impossible to estimate how many people are helped to maintain their health by their faith, though this is undoubtedly a form of spiritual healing. One has seen some people with an evident gift of faith and prayer for healing, and some remarkable results. I know a woman who suffered terribly from arthritis, wrapped herself in self-pity and retired from life. There came into her life a great spiritual experience which turned her decisively to Christ in faith and surrender. The self-pity went, and the negative thoughts about herself which for years had lowered her vitality, a new spirit took possession of her—and most of the arthritis disappeared! An older person was badly hurt in an accident and a broken hip resulted: the bone would not knit, a stool with rollers on it provided the only means of locomotion in the house and there could be no venturing forth on the street. Then someone with faith said, "I believe God could cause

[4] *The Art of Ministering to the Sick,* pp. 63-64.

that bone to knit if we prayed about it." Pray they did, and the bone did knit, and the person walks everywhere without difficulty—though the person in whom this healing took place was above seventy years of age.

The most amazing healing I ever saw was in Dr. F. Le-Roy Satterlee, one of the last survivors of the original X-ray experimenters, and a member of my parish and Vestry.[5] He suffered with skin-cancer for forty years. His heart had enlarged from a normal size of six and a half inches across to nine and one quarter inches; and gave him intense and terrible pain. One night when he thought he was dying, he prayed to God for four hours—not that he would live, but that he would find God beyond any doubt. After this he fell asleep, slept for six hours (which he had not done for years) and wakened knowing that in some part he was healed. His heart, by measurement taken scientifically, had gone back to normal size. His pain from cancer greatly lessened. The last year of his life was especially fruitful, both spiritually and in inventions. I was with him when a healing took place in his feet, which were perfectly stiff but which, as we prayed before the altar simply giving thanks for his conversion and partial healing, became very much more limber. This was only a partial healing, I repeat, but it was a very amazing one. Taking place in a scientist, who came at the whole matter experimentally, it was peculiarly moving and convincing.

The mystery remains: why is not spiritual healing more frequent? And to it I know no answer. I have seen devout and believing and committed people ask for healing, but it was not always vouchsafed to them. St. Paul prayed for his "thorn in the flesh," that it might be taken from him. Surely he had faith, and was worthy, and fulfilled the requirements so far as we can understand them. Yet the

[5] I give here his own account, and his own interpretation: not my own only.

reply that came to his prayers was not healing, it was the tremendous truth, "My grace is sufficient for thee: for my strength is made perfect in weakness."[6] Like all prayer, the final result of the prayer for healing must be left to God and His infinite wisdom. To hold out a promise that someone will surely be healed if they pray and have others pray for them, is perhaps to raise a hope that may not be satisfied, with the result of great disappointment and possible loss of faith. Better far to pray much for and with them, helping them to open their minds and bodies to the inflow of the healing tides of God, but not requiring any particular outcome to the prayer.[7] And we must not forget the constant gift of health to many people, the two sources of which are obedience to God's laws of health and the kind of faith that keeps the mind and heart and will pointed at all times to God.

Ordinarily a very sick person lays hold of faith by two handles: their own need, and the faith of other people. Great weakness or much pain prevent complete or serious wrestling with the questions of religion, or laying hold upon faith in the thorough fashion elsewhere spoken about in this book. But we must watch, too, for exceptions to this rule. A skeptical magazine writer, twice divorced and an alcoholic, fetched up in Ward M of Bellevue Hospital, New York, with cancer. He knew what faith was, but had never made his peace with God. He knew how sick he was and what ordeal faced him. Visiting him one day I said, "You are a well educated man and you have read a lot; but I think your best reading days are ahead of you. Just for information, why don't you begin to read the Bible? Start in just like any other book, and see what it says." He

[6] II Corinthians 12:9.

[7] A Catholic priest, asked what was the greatest miracle he ever saw at Lourdes, said, "The look of resignation and faith on the faces of those who were not healed."

walked down the ward with me, took the Bible from the shelf where it stood by itself, and began to read. It interested him. He read for three and four hours a day in it, and always had a list of questions to ask me about it when I came. God touched him through the Bible, and he found his Lord and his faith. Through more than a year of mounting agony, he kept a living faith in God, a vital stream of prayer going up and grace coming down, that was a most powerful witness to all the people about him, some of whom he led to faith in that last year. The sickness made him face the seriousness of life; the pain and the anticipation of more of it, made him seek for help; the Bible filled his mind with a new set of truths and values— and God plus the fellowship of some people who believed in God did the rest.

Faith is the one thing that gives sick people fundamental help. If the doctors can bring about physical cure, they have done a great service; but if they cannot, there is nothing more which, as doctors, they can do. But faith not only helps on the cure if cure is possible: faith makes possible the bearing of pain, and it gives an assurance that goes beyond death. There is a Christian way to do everything, and there is a Christian way to get sick. "The pain God is allowed to guide"[8] may be a great blessing to the sufferer. Dr. Richard Cabot says, "In my own life it is *suffering,* frustration, humiliation, grief, remorse, that have best nourished growth. . . . As we look back along the path of our lives, do we not see our sufferings as our best teachers? Especially if those sufferings did not have to be borne alone. 'Man's extremity is God's opportunity' to teach what we are too stupid, too self-satisfied, too habit-bound, to grasp at other times."[9]

[8] See II Cor. 7:10 (Moffatt's translation).
[9] *The Art of Ministering to the Sick,* pp. 17-18.

IX

Helping the Mentally Sick

HAS MENTAL SICKNESS greatly increased in our time, or has our awareness of mental sickness increased? The question cannot be answered with final authority. But its probable answer is that both mental sickness and our awareness of it have increased in recent years. In an editorial[1] *The Christian Century* comments: "Mental diagnosis of draftees by psychiatrists has resulted in the rejection of 1,340,000 men, two-thirds of whom were found mentally defective and the other third deficient (including illiterates). These rejectees on mental grounds constitute 35 per cent of all draftees classified as unfit for military service. Even after this screening out of mental cases before induction, 216,000 inductees have been discharged from the army (up to February 1, 1944) on neuropsychiatric grounds; and this is two-thirds as many as have been discharged for wounds or other physical causes. All these figures for mental defectives are much greater than those for the last war. Perhaps the psychic condition of the nation is worse. Perhaps the diagnosis is more rigid. Or perhaps, the psychiatrists now for the first time having a chance on a large scale to apply their new science, are having a field day."

About a third of the casualties returned from the war have been neuropsychiatric—a larger proportion than the armed forces expected, but not larger than the psychiatrists

[1] July 26, 1944.

expected. There are no bones broken, perhaps no wound-scars visible; but there are some terrible mental dislocations, some terrible wounds in the mind. These men are different from what they were before—some utterly changed, apathetic; some highly nervous, intolerant in discussion; some with repetitious nightmares, headaches, periods of forgetfulness, tremors etc.—obviously sick. Others will not be noticeably sick, but they will be irritable, jittery, demanding, self-centered, dissatisfied, unable to settle down to routine. Some of these men must be cared for in hospitals by medical and psychiatric doctors, some for longer or shorter periods, some for good. They will need visits from family, friends, ministers, who will be welcomed by the hospital if they coöperate with what the doctors are trying to accomplish. Many of these men have already been sent out of the hospitals, not because they were fully ready for normal civilian life, but from sheer pressure on the capacity of the hospitals and on the physicians' time. Few of us will be without some contact with those who have been shocked by the war.

And all of us who want to help people will sooner or later find ourselves trying to help someone who does not react in a normal way to life either mentally or emotionally. Some are physical defectives, and the family must decide whether they can best be taken care of at home or in an institution. Others are so seriously sick mentally that they are virtually insane, and should be put into the hands of physicians and basically cared for by them, with such assistance from lay-people as the doctors may think advantageous to the patients. Others suffer from mental or emotional disturbances in which they may need the help of doctors or psychiatrists, but in which unprofessional friends can be of large assistance if these friends will trouble to learn something about how to deal with them. We rule ourselves out as able to be of any assistance at all if we do not realize the reality and suffering of mental sickness, or if we think there is any use in saying to those who suffer from these non-physical ailments, "Buck up and snap out of it!" In various degrees, and with various possibilities of cure, these people are sick. The mind gets sick just as the body does. One can no more cure a sick mind by a sudden determination of will than one can heal a broken leg. It is a longer, more serious process.

In order that we better understand the nature of this kind of sickness, I am going to quote somewhat at length from a book called *The Neurotic Personality of our Time,* by Dr. Karen Horney: "Neurotics are different from the average individuals in their reactions . . . two characteristics which one may discern in all neuroses without having an intimate knowledge of the personality structure: a certain rigidity in reaction and a discrepancy between potentialities and accomplishments . . . the neurotic has the impression that he stands in his own way . . . one essential factor common to all neuroses, and that is anxieties and the defenses built up against them . . . the neurotic is invariably a suffering person . . . another essential characteristic of a neurosis . . . the presence of conflicting tendencies of the existence of which, or at least the precise content of which, the neurotic is himself unaware . . . a neurosis is a psychic disturbance brought about by fears and defenses against these fears, and by attempts to find compromise solutions for conflicting tendencies."

Dr. Horney gives reasons for speaking of the "neurotic personality of our time," drawing the distinction between "situation neuroses" and "character neuroses," the latter being one in which "the main disturbance lies in the deformation of character . . . in speaking of the neurotic personality of our time, I not only mean that there are neurotic persons having essential peculiarities in common, but also that these basic similarities are essentially produced by the difficulties existing in our time and culture." The following are given as trends of the neurotics of this time:

(1) Excessive dependence on the approval or affection of others.
(2) Inner insecurity, feelings of inferiority and inadequacy.
(3) Definite inhibitions, e.g., in expressing wishes, taking a stand, knowing what they want; incapacity to play.
(4) Acts of going against someone, "aggression".
(5) Compulsive need for sex, or inhibition about it.

Dr. Horney speaks about "the basic anxiety" as a feeling of loneliness and helplessness in a hostile world; and says that "fear is a reaction that is proportionate to the danger one has to face, whereas anxiety is a disproportionate reaction to danger, or even a reaction to imaginary danger . . . but in the case of fear the danger is a transparent, objective one and in the case of anxiety, it is hidden and subjective." Our culture has four ways of escaping anxiety: rationalize it; deny it; narcotize it; avoid thoughts, feelings, impulses and situations which might arouse it. We take four principal ways to protect ourselves against "the basic anxiety": affection, submissiveness, power and withdrawal.

Now when we set out to help people who suffer from such neuroses, we must remember that we want to help them to become over a period of time, if possible, very different kinds of people. This is hard in the case of a normal person, it is much harder in the case of a person who is neurotic. I quote Dr. Horney again, "To make any changes in a developed personality is extremely hard for everyone. But for the neurotic person this task is twice as hard, not only because he has a greater difficulty in recognizing the necessity for change but also because so many of his attitudes are necessitated by anxiety."[2] For a normal

2 *Ibid.*, p. 246.

person to change may require a great deal of uprooting of the Old Adam, stirring lazy stumps to alter old and comfortable habits; but he can generally see the desirability of changing, and know that he would be better off if he were changed: whereas the neurotic feels helpless in the presence of a challenge to change, he feels that not only is he incapable of making any change, but that a change would rob him of the few inner moorings and securities which he possesses—therefore he resists any change with a kind of anticipated dread and despair, often with heated self-justification.

It needs to be said again and again: such people can only be understood with great sympathy, and they can only be helped with great patience. Do not attempt to help one of them if you are not prepared for a long road, for few signs of progress and many set-backs, and if you are not ready to spend yourself generously and painstakingly for what may look like a meagre result. Unless you feel genuinely sorry for them, and are prepared to keep on long after your emotional pity seems to have been exhausted, do not tackle it at all. You will have to listen again and again to what is basically the same pattern of story: but these rehearsals which are tiresome to the listener are of great therapeutic value to the teller. There is no place for, "Yes, you told me all that before" or "We have been over that"—for the going over it again and again is what lightens the burden of it for him.

In the case of any but the most undeveloped cases of negative thinking, we shall be most unwise if we attempt to work without a good psychologist or psychiatrist. Even clergy with some experience have had disastrous results sometimes from attempting to deal unprofessionally with what is fundamentally a sickness which requires professional skill. Try to find a psychiatrist who believes in the Christian religion, or at least one who recognizes its power to clarify people's thinking and help them in their living; and urge the sick person to go for a consultation. Then find out from the doctor how you, as a friend, can assist him in what he wants to accomplish for the patient. He will be glad to have you help him in most cases, provided he finds you will work in such a way as to supplement and not contradict what he is trying to accomplish. No layman understands these things as thoroughly as a trained doctor. We may bring in supplementary help such as he cannot provide: but where a person is sick enough to consult a physician, he is sick enough to follow the physician's orders and regimen; and we shall best help him if we build up his confidence in his doctor, supplementing this by faith.

Many people are mentally and emotionally sick because they demand of themselves, of others, and of life, a perfection which none of us ever quite sees in this world, and toward which we move only by some exertion on our own part. The world is full of people who want to have Utopia by next Friday. The 'economic planners' are going to have an economic Utopia, the educators are going to have an educational Utopia, the religious are going to have the Kingdom of God on earth—all these things, of course, provided their own scheme is followed. Those who are too impractical or too impatient to do anything about bringing this Utopia an actual mite nearer by helping actual people to do a better job of actual living, sometimes retire and write big books about Utopia. Ideas are so much better behaved than people—they stay put in the right place in a paragraph so much better than people stay put in the right frame of mind, and books can be such a shiningly perfect picture of Utopia, while people are forever falling short of it in some way. Visions are wonderful to have, provided we have the gumption to follow after them long enough to make some real progress in reaching them. The success of life does not lie wholly in the bigness or perfection of its visions: it lies also in its patient and plodding determination to realize its visions at least in some actual measure.

All this means that life does not consist in dreaming about perfection, but in travelling towards it. That is, life is struggle; and from that struggle no one is exempt. The struggle arises out of our warfare with imperfection as we seek to turn it towards perfection. All real living is therefore a kind of conflict. It is of no use for psychologists or ministers to tell people that if they understand themselves psychologically, or discover a real faith, they will be free from conflict. There are only two lots of people that are free from conflict: those who live entirely in a world of make-believe, and those in cemeteries. Life is constantly putting us into fresh situations which, however at peace we may be inside when we reach them, throw us into fresh conflict. To be free from conflict would be to be free from life. There are some conflicts that are tied into the very weave of life: the conflict between age and youth, between man and woman, between convictions and tolerance, between self-interest and service, between realism and optimism, between contentment and ambition, between self and society—the list is endlessly long. Each of these things is in some measure essential, and each is in some measure in conflict with some opposite that is also essential. Conflict badly met, or conflict which seems incapable of being resolved, leads to frustration.

What we *can* say to people is that they can make their conflicts creative and not destructive. The important thing about a person's life is not the number nor intensity of his conflicts, but what he does with his conflicts. Personal conflict courageously and creatively and wisely met can lead to far more than merely personal victory. Many a good work of art has been produced by men forced to write or paint to keep the wolf from the door. The newspaper man's "deadline" which puts him in conflict, knowing he must have a thousand words written by a certain time, pushes many a recalcitrant sentence off the end of his pen. Frustration met with common sense and turned to constructive ends is a good deal like steam which, instead of escaping wastefully in the air, is applied to the pistons of an engine. John Wesley and Abraham Lincoln were without doubt two of the greatest men of the 18th and 19th centuries; both of them were married to difficult wives who must have caused them infinite private grief; but there may have been a connection between that personal frustration and the urge which drove Wesley to cover England with a new spiritual awakening, and which drove Lincoln to pour out his compassionate spirit in a concern for humankind which is one of the great treasures of the race.

This push and pull of one force against another, one value against another, is what makes a sense of proportion so needful in life. That is why no one will ever quite understand life without a sense of humor, which is a sense of proportion. It is why Christ so often spoke in paradox, "He that saveth his life shall lose it," and why no one can pursue one truth all the time without remembering at the same time its complementary truth, unless he wants to be a fanatic. The patient balancing of values, seeing life steadily and seeing it whole, must be the aim of the mentally sick.

We shall help them most if we can combine in our relation to them an awareness of what they are suffering, with a great hope, a great faith and a great caring. "I believe you can do it," should be the pervasive, underlying attitude we take towards them, because nine-tenths of the time they are convinced that they cannot do it. Seldom should we give them a direct challenge concerning their short-comings: this wounds and discourages more than it heals or helps. Our challenges should take the form of seeing next steps which they should take, drawing this out of themselves if possible, talking over with them how best to do it, and helping them to take the step. For mentally sick people to make decisions, to act, to go among people, to make a considerate judgment, require the same kind of effort as it takes for a little child to talk, to walk, to put together a puzzle, to go out to strangers—and must be backed by the same kind of encouragement. When one's emotions seem paralyzed, it is a superhuman effort to pick up one's room, to keep accounts, to go and buy a suit of clothes, to make any kind of move or decision. But each step taken is a point gained. Progress does not come by dreaming of how things ought to be in a wished-for future : it comes by taking the one next step indicated.

This is the only way to tackle the very common problem of inferiority. A decision, an act, even if it be a failure, constitutes progress; whereas thinking about the act leads to thoughts of incapacity which put a person back instead of forward. People who are not in full control of their inner lives learn to control them by taking small, immediate, possible steps. For instance, a person who has grown very dependent on the help of another reaches the time when this ought to be lessened if not cut short, because the sympathy which was meant to strengthen has begun to hinder and unman. The relationships should not be broken —that is generally hurtful—but the degree of dependence definitely lessened. The suggestion of this to the sick person will probably produce fear and strong resistance. "But I can't get along—I just can't go on!" will be the frenzied remonstrance. We should have talked the matter over if possible with the doctor; and if he agrees with us, we must lovingly, persistently stand by our point. When this is done in the loving confidence that this next step means progress and that now they can go forward with more assurance, there will be sure gain.

But all new steps like this must be put up to mentally

sick people, not as stern, hard challenges, but as natural, possible next moves. We must talk about them cheerfully, encouragingly. In the case of people normal in the main, we need to remember that much sickness today is mixed up with sin, and may have come in part from persisting in some kind of wrong-doing, so that we need to be morally alert and challenging; but in the case of those who are not normal, it is sometimes true that whatever wrong they do is so much mixed with the sickness itself that we must be very compassionate and understanding. We must try not to inculcate deeper feelings of guilt in neurotic people. They are there already, in far too great measure. I quote Dr. Horney again, "Guilt feelings, like inferiority feelings, are not at all unwelcome (to the neurotic): the neurotic person is far from eager to get rid of them. In fact he insists on his guilt and vigorously resists every attempt to exonerate him."[3] Neurotics will sit smilingly and call themselves by the most fearful names; but this does not concern something about which they really feel badly, or mean to do anything: it is a bid for attention, for sympathy, for approval, even for admiration! Moods of guilt can only do harm: steps away from self-centered irresponsibility can only help. To see, and help them see, what the steps ought to be—not condemning themselves for not paying their bills, but going and paying the grocer this afternoon—not reproaching themselves for not answering letters, but taking five, seven, ten letters on the desk and answering them today—not wishing vainly they were of more use, but going this evening to call on that sick or shut-in friend—and to help them take this actual step—this is to be helpful to the mentally and emotionally sick.

People like this will want to see us often, and we must be prepared to see them often, especially in the earlier stages which may last a year or two. A definite appointment—

[3] *Ibid.,* p. 232.

"three weeks from Monday at four o'clock"—gives them something to hold on to in the meantime, and to prepare for so that the talk may cover the points in their minds and be made most fruitful; whereas to say "I'll see you sometime soon" gives them an insecure feeling. There are certain things towards which we should aim in our interviews with people like this:

(a) a sense of unhurried leisure, so that they are not pushed.
(b) a positive, loving attitude which will not be discouraged, and is never "through," no matter what happens.
(c) a readiness to hear the same essential story over and over again.
(d) a clear-headed objective understanding of the person himself, so that mistaken diagnoses or unreal fears are discarded.

A young woman was in great distress of mind. She had no philosophy of life, got on badly with the family, and had tried suicide. She was taken into the house of an older woman whom she had come to trust. When a difficult time came on, she would ask to see the older woman, and talk it out. The older woman was not a trained psychologist, but she was a Christian and a woman of the world with experience and good sense. They would talk it out, and sometimes pray about it. Slowly faith began coming to this girl, not all at once. Former unhappy associations of religion gave way to happy and positive ones. She began going to church. She found and made friends. She reached out to other lonely, distressed, mixed-up people, and found she could help them. She is now giving her whole time to helping such people in a kind of "sanitarium without walls." She is useful and growingly happy.

Spiritual help for people like this needs to be of two kinds: time for personal talks, and then exposure to the objective side of religion. Meetings where people speak with freedom of their problems and the answers God is giving them are of the utmost help to reasonably normal people; but they will sometimes put a person who is sick in mind on a kind of tension—he will feel it incumbent on him to speak in this way, or to have a glorious experience like that one who just spoke—whereas he feels utterly incapable of any such thing. It is the objective, as against the subjective, factors of religion that offer to such people a mooring and an anchor. A young woman of ability has been going to a psychiatrist for some time. He helps her to understand herself and make her adjustments. She needs a religious support as well, and goes regularly to church. She finds security and strength in the Holy Communion, where her own emotions are not to the fore, but where the grace of God may be objectively laid hold upon. She finds help in services, through the regular liturgy. These things become like concrete bars on which she can lay hold and pull herself out from self-centeredness, depression and fear. One can watch, over a period of time, and see the actual difference which this kind of strength makes when poured into a person who is unsure of herself. Slowly the referring of every situation to the way it strikes 'her,' and the turning of conversation to her ailments, gives way to more outgoing care for other people. One sees how much of mental sickness is self-centeredness, and how every step away from self towards God and other people is a direct boon.

Soon people like this can begin reaching out to help others like themselves. They should do it with some supervision and help from a doctor or minister, but as soon as the sensitiveness which has been burned up in self-analysis and self-pity begins to be controlled, so that it can be turned outwards in sympathy and service, it should be done. I have had some real success in referring mentally sick people to those who have begun to get well, and of whose character and judgment I am sure: it has been a blessing both ways.

No one can understand like someone who has 'been there' and yet found it is not necessary to 'stay there.' The friendship and fellowship which develops between such people can be of the utmost benefit to them both. They will usually need the continued help of doctor or minister, especially where a knotty problem arises, or when both of them get 'sunk' at the same time. But they can do much for each other. The therapy of talking matters out, which as we have insisted so often must be repeated many times, saves the time of doctor or other professional adviser, yet has equal value if the advice given is in line with the therapy which he recommends. So great is the power of these people to help one another that a well-known doctor in New York said to me that he thought there ought to be a "Neurotics Anonymous" which would function like "Alcoholics Anonymous." As cured alcoholics are best able to help other alcoholics to be cured, so neurotics that are on the way to cure may be the best people to point the way for other neurotics. They understand each other, they enjoy being plunged into human "situations" and difficulties. Beginning with the love of immature people to be understood, and moving on themselves towards a greater maturity, they will want to understand others. Perhaps maturity consists in little more than the transformation of the passion to be understood into the passion to understand.

There is one curious fact that anyone who has dealt with mentally sick or neurotic people will have observed: and that is the compensation of nature in giving to those who are in some part deficient an added competence in another direction. Often they are keen-minded and possessed of insight. They have been sharpened by their own suffering into a keener perception of trouble, suffering, need, in other people. So often I have noticed how natural is the spiritual faculty in them. It is as if they felt such need within as told them that it would not find satisfaction in anything that derives entirely from this world, but only from the highest Source of all. Prayer is not only a source of eventual power, it is a source of great present relief, once the whole story has been brought out into the light. Prayer is not a substitute for the patient listening on our part which allows the person to say what is on his heart, and to acquaint us with the real nature of the problem. With how many burdened, afflicted people, in despair about themselves, afraid to venture forth again into a life they neither asked for nor understand, have I knelt in a few moments of quiet prayer in my study, and seen the prayer roll back the cloud of depression, of fear, of anxiety, as a cool breeze in the summer will blow away the humidity of a sultry day! Seldom have I had to urge this, or explain about it: a few concrete instances of what prayer has done for people, and it is natural to slip down on our knees, and to let God, by His Presence and power, break the tension and bring fresh hope in its place. This opens up a new avenue of experiment and discovery, which can be pursued alone or wherever they may be; and of which the results are assured.

From some kinds of mental and emotional disturbance people may expect to be practically completely free: it is like a sickness from which there is recovery. From other kinds the release is never complete—they are like a person who will walk with a stiff leg for life after an injury to his knee. The families and friends of such people need great understanding and patience, such as it is hoped a book like this can help to bring them. All who would help them must keep the positive picture, working always with them in love and in faith, knowing the infinite possibilities of human nature as progressively it is infused with the Spirit of God. Sudden miracles in the mental area are suspect: the sound growth is the slow kind.

But I would emphasize the assistance which all of us

can bring, or can be trained and helped to bring, to mentally sick people. Friendliness, 'personalness,' caring, interest, the giving of time and the sharing of their burdens and problems—these things are the incalculables and imponderables of helping them, which no chart can quite measure. Recently I have seen someone seriously sick in mind greatly helped by the modern 'shock' treatment, and through being given expert care in one of our great mental hospitals. What *really* did it—the shock-treatment, the nursing care, the family's patient understanding, the faith for which the Church and the minister stood—or all these things, plus perhaps some others which are unknown? I quote Dr. Alexander Reid Martin,[4] "Where there has been recovery following accidents, severe illnesses and 'shock' treatment, the prolonged nursing care and the increase in human interest necessitated by the physical condition introduce important human factors which have never been properly evaluated. More and more it is being realised that this human factor plays the important curative rôle." We must read, study, observe, talk with experienced people, and so gain all the insight and knowledge we can have for this supremely important work; they will help us in what to do, and often in what not to do. But because of the importance of what Dr. Martin calls the "human factor," any of us may find himself or herself highly useful in helping mentally sick people to find their way back to health.

Amid the stresses of the world into which we are moving, it is not likely that mental sickness will decrease: it is far more likely that it will increase. The mental hospitals are crowded now. The war has created many more. We must work ardently for two things: one, the adequate care and relief of those who now suffer from mental sickness;

[4] *Recent Trends in Psychiatry of Particular Significance for Religion,* Federal Council of the Churches of Christ in America, p. 14.

and two, the creation of such an outlook on life as will cut down the proportion of mental sickness as steadily as possible. Fundamentally this seems to me to mean the spread of living, working faith. People who really believe in God have a Power to turn to in the hour of their own need, and a cause into which to throw their energies, which together spell the probability of mental health.

X

Helping the Fearful

NOT LONG AGO I was talking with a doctor who said that there seems to be some universal deficiency in the modern make-up which leads to fatigue. This same fatigue afflicts civilians as often besets men at war. As yet, this doctor said, it does not seem clear just what this fatigue comes from—whether it is a chemical deficiency, or an emotional one, perhaps a chemical one which causes the emotional one. Research is being done in the matter, and may reveal the secret.

Meantime one may venture the belief that at least a contributing cause to this deficiency is the kind of lowered vitality which comes from some kind of fear. There is a vast amount of fear abroad in the world today—not fear that the war will be lost, for that fear is behind us, but fear that the vast sacrifice of the war may be in vain (a very legitimate fear), fear that we may lose someone that is dear to us, fear of what kind of world we are heading into, fear about our own security. To these fears that arise out of the conditions of our time must be added the deep and ancient dreads that man has felt since the dawn of consciousness—fear of his own safety and preservation in a cold universe, fear of not making enough impression as he goes through the world and gaining recognition, fear of pain and illness, fear of old age, fear of death and the unknown beyond. There are people who, looking at the whole experience of existence itself, are like children looking into a dark room: their reaction is one of flight. It is *life,* in all its totality, that many people are afraid of. "Tired of livin' and feared of dyin'," as Ole Man River says. Perhaps this should be more correctly called 'anxiety.' Berdyaev makes the distinction between fear "which has causes" and "is connected with danger, and with the every day world of common experience;" and anguish *(angst)* which is experienced, "not in the face of empirical danger, but in confronting the mystery of being and non-being, when face to face with the transcendent abyss, in the face of the unknown."[1]

If we are to help people who suffer from fear, we must understand fear and we must realize that even where fear concerns something wholly unreal which does not exist, the *fear* exists and is as definite as pain. Our leisure, our education, even our psychological knowledge, have given us time and tools to increase the number of our brooding fears. Go down behind the outward things in many lives today, and what do you find underlying them, down in the unconscious where we manufacture the real emotional urges of life? Instead of the well of confidence and courage and faith which should be there to draw on, there is often a well of fear. Instead of an unconscious stored with experiences and evidences that arise from meeting life with assurance and success, there is an unconscious full of nameless and haunting fears against which the conscious life is often waging a ceaseless and a losing battle. People love to haunt the doctors' offices, because they hope that there may be some pill, some operation, some rest-cure, some psychological analysis, which will do away with fear. But none of these things can quite do it. The fears that are generating and multiplying like rats in the cellar of our minds are emotional, impalpable. They can only be met by emotional and impalpable medicine,—medicine of the mind, medicine of controlled thinking and emotion.

[1] *Slavery and Freedom,* p. 52.

How You Can Help Other People

We need always to remember that fear has its uses. Like opium and alcohol, it would not be here if it did not have a function. Fear was given to man for his protection. There are things in life which ought to be feared. We are glad to inculcate in our children the fear of leaning out of an open window, or running in front of a car. Pain should lead to fear which leads to precaution and calling the doctor. Deadly germs, fast-moving traffic, the accumulation of unmet responsibilities, the poison of negative thinking—these things are meant to be feared. They are objective and it is reasonable to fear that which can destroy us. If we fear the right things, we shall be better able to stop fearing the wrong ones. The twelfth chapter of St. Luke contains a perfect category of the things to fear, and the things not to fear. We are not to fear death or being killed, we are not to fear being called on the carpet for our faith, we are not to fear that our bodily wants will not be supplied, and we are not to fear for the future, either our own or that of God's cause in the world. But we are to fear the everlasting consequences of the kind of life we live, we are to fear blasphemy against the Holy Spirit, and we are to fear meanness about money and possessions.

Where fear has not gone to a dangerous point, it is usually found in conjunction with some other problem. Someone has lost a job and is looking for another—that is the chief problem—fear of not finding a job is just an accompaniment. Someone is poorly and sick and the doctor says an operation is indicated—their worry is the operation, pain, expense, etc., and the fear is only a kind of accessory to the operation. A man looks forward to marriage, and all seems an excited anticipation—until someone with trust and understanding gets it out of him that he is very much afraid of marriage, is not sure he can make a go of it, perhaps would give anything at times if he could withdraw from it altogether. Sometimes one has to look for the fear

[150]

in connection with other problems; for fear makes them seem more serious, and holds us back from finding their answer and solution.

When fear is more developed, it may appear more readily to the person himself as the major problem. When fear has been present a good while, it congeals and solidifies into frustration. Frustration is fear without hope and without relief, fear accepted as a fate and not regarded as a problem. Frustration is the condition of those who have not sufficient talent, personality, strength, health of the whole self, to achieve their normal ambitions. It uses up the emotions needed for the prosecution of life, and spends them in wasteful, fruitless brooding. Such a round of fear and frustration, from which there seems no tangent of escape, is the fertile source of nervous break-downs. The body cannot carry its own burdens, plus the lowered vitality resulting from mental and emotional waste; and so it gives way.

The best place to prevent the development of early fears, and so of a tendency towards fear all through life, is, of course, the home into which a child is born. Children that from the first are loved and wanted and properly cared for are healthy, secure children. But children that are not wanted, and discover the fact, suffer from the profoundest insecurity which can be known. Even very little children react like delicate seismographs to the shock of conflict and unhappiness about them. Children that do not have love and affection from their parents are being robbed of one of the great defenses against constitutional fear. Divorce, which causes in children not only bewilderment and shame, but a division in loyalty and affection, and often a fear of of what is to become of them, runs up a large bill which the future must pay. Society is going to reap the results in divided, neurotic personalities, unable to carry their full share, some of them having to be cared for entirely. A high percentage of men discharged from military service on psychological grounds come from broken homes. The chief consideration where divorce is contemplated should not be the comfort nor convenience of either party, but the welfare of the children. Unhappily married people often say that it tears their children to pieces to live in the midst of obvious uncongeniality and unhappiness. True: but why do they not realize that a spiritual change in one or both parents would begin to bring about a change in atmosphere, that God would make a difference in the home—whereas divorce puts the situation forever beyond cure? The best way to prevent fear in the hearts of our growing children is to marry on a Christian basis, with God right at the heart of the relationship from the first, with a permanent loyalty accepted as beyond question, and with children regarded as a blessing from God. On such a basis our children will be brought up with the minimum of fear.

Yet from somewhere fear creeps in. Negative suggestions come from other people, from the talk of other children, from the very experience of living itself. We cannot wholly prevent fear. The next thing to do is to try to cure it. How can we help people suffering from fear?

1. We can help them to articulate their fears, and get them into the open. Fear that lives in the dark places of our minds is like the thoughts that sometimes haunt us at night—it is magnified by the shadows in which it lives. Let it come into the open, so that another hears it, so that it has been voiced in words—and it will begin to appear a little less formidable. A person begins with a shy smile by saying, "This may sound very foolish to you, but you know sometimes I feel I simply can't go into a crowd of people at all: and sometimes I wonder if I am losing my mind, I get so confused and forget people's names, and feel I have nothing to say to them." Everything depends on how we respond to such an overture. If we say, "Why, I

love people, I can't understand anybody fearing to go among them," we shall forfeit any possibility of helping him. But if we say, "There is nothing foolish about that— I sometimes feel afraid when I have to speak in public, and a little weary with certain people—I quite understand how you feel," it will give him the confidence to say more. Get him to tell you when it happened last, and how he felt and all about it. He will hardly believe it of a well-adjusted person, but let him know your own shyness and fears, and tell him just how you have felt, so he will know you are not manufacturing something to assist him. The more fully it all comes out into the open, the more relief it will give him, and the more diagnosis it will give you about him.

2. If the fear appears to be of a very serious and psychopathic kind, it would be well to get the person into the hands of a good doctor. Once I talked with a man whose problems gave every appearance of being simple and moral and conscious: but as I got deeper, it was as if I had put my hand down what looked like a mole-hole, and found it was a cavern. The thing was much more deep-seated and complex and the man was much sicker in his mind than at first I suspected. It took a good psychiatrist and myself several years to get him straightened out. There is nothing to fear about seeking to help such a man: we cannot harm him by sympathy, by letting him talk to us, by sharing our own experience with him and helping him on to such faith as we have. But some fear, appearing outwardly only as exaggerated inferiority, can lead on to such depression as will threaten suicide; or perhaps the mind will seek release in a world of fancy which may unhinge it from reality altogether and cause insanity. Sympathy, common-sense and experience will help us to recognize this more serious type of fear; and to call in appropriate help.

3. We must help people to look their fears right in the face. There are dogs that you can keep at bay even when

they are angry, if you keep your eyes looking straight into their eyes. And fears are like that. "I am afraid I am going to die." Well, let's consider that : the Christian faith believes that what lies beyond is a good deal better than what is here. All the people that have ever lived before our time have had to face death. Nothing which is so natural can be too frightening. I knew a woman desperately afraid of death all her days : she had a goitre, and it brought her right up to the doorway of death; then she began getting well, and she never feared death again, because when she got right up against it, she found she was not afraid. Or someone says, "I have got to face my new boss and a whole new office force on Monday, and I am panicky about it." Well, did you ever think, every one of the employes there had a 'first day' like you? The boss himself had a 'first time' when he dictated letters to a secretary, and probably his throat was dry and the letters were stilted. Don't think about them as a mass of critical, unfriendly people : think of them as a series of ordinary individuals, with fears of their own. The more you go out to them, forgetful of yourself, the more they will go out to you forgetful of anything except that a polite and friendly person has come to join the force. We almost always tend to push fears away from us, and not to consider them. This way they increase and intensify. The right thing to do is to take them right down off the shelf, handle them, look them over, take their measure, and remember that many others have faced these fears and worse and overcome them.

4. Many people who suffer from fear feel that life itself is hopelessly complex, and they do not know where to begin to take hold of it. The more I watch life and people, the more do I feel that the complexity lies, not in the life, but in the people. Life is a game which cannot be played unless you know the rules; but I do not believe life is just a snarl and a tangle. We often find ourselves in complex situations.

But how many times have we sinned ourselves into that complexity? When a man does not know what to do about a wife to whom he has promised his life-long loyalty, and another woman with whom he has fallen violently in love, it is not to the complexity of life that he must charge up his confusion, but to the vagaries of his own affectional life. When a man, through desire to make his mother comfortable in her old age, borrows so heavily that he runs himself into a staggering debt, his difficulty is not due to the complexity of existence, but to the folly of thinking there is any real kindness in that kind of extravagance. Life begins to get complex—does it not?—when we leave the pretty well established old moorings, and go off on moral ventures which defy the experience of the past and assume that we are 'different' and can somehow 'beat the game.' The way out of this kind of fear is a simple, direct, honest moral appraisal of the situation—facing all the facts without flinching. Then clear up wrongs so far as possible—break off the relation with the other woman, acknowledge the debt and promise to begin paying it off as rapidly as possible. Take hold of the thing by the end of some moral string, and it will unravel. If you run away from the situation on the basis that life is impossibly complex, you may find yourself seeing no way out but suicide.

5. Of course, the antithesis to fear is faith. It is what the fearful person would give anything to have. We must help him bring that "anything" down out of the clouds of the impossible on to the ground of actual experimental steps. A woman came in great need. She was the unmarried daughter who had stayed at home with an ageing mother; and when the mother went, the annuity went. She had been brought up without a skill. She was in the middle fifties. She had nothing but the tradition of a conventional belief. All right. We went to work on that! "You believe in God, don't you?" Yes, she believed there was a God. "Then

He cares about what happens to His children, doesn't He?" Yes, she thought He probably did—but that didn't show her what to do about next month's rent. "If He is intelligent, He has always a plan, hasn't He—not just an ideal Will that a person might miss and go beyond forever, but a Plan for them now, today, in their situation?" Well, it sounded reasonable. "But how do you find that Plan?" she asked. The answer was, "First you have got to get into touch with God himself. And that means we must let down all the barriers on our side. Sin is anything that stands between us and God. So that fear is not just a problem, it's also a sin, and we have got to get rid of it just as much as a drunkard must get rid of his drink." That was a challenge. The fear was given over to God. Faith began to fill its place. She began reading her Bible, coming to church, making contact with people who were also trying the experiment of faith. Faith does not swoop down in automatic deliverance to people, like a rain-storm in a drought. People work for faith, climb the steps to it, earn it and win it by reasonable stages. She was lifted steadily out of that fear into an atmosphere of faith which has never left her. There have been trials to face, problems to solve, needs to be met: but a living God has cancelled fear.

But such faith as this is not always so smoothly won as by the woman we have just told about. A letter lies in my desk which says, "Unless God and I can form a treaty or something—get together on things—I'm going to be wiped out sure as hell. I keep grasping around (quite sincerely), but I always feel the big, important thing has evaded me somehow. . . . Frankly, I'm just as afraid of God as I am of a bolt of lightning—and that's no help." I believe that such fear as this arises from an acute sense of failure and self-judgment which has been carried over and projected on God—so that God has become a kind of magnified Conscience, a huge, demanding Power that threatens to annihilate us because of the impossibility of our attaining what He asks of us.

There are two things which I want to say to such a person.

The first is that self-hatred is as great a sin as self-love. It may be a deeper sin and an even more destructive one. Self-love is a preoccupation with oneself which is at least positive : self-hatred is a preoccupation with oneself which is negative, destructive, doomed to disaster. No God can want to see this. We must try to burst through the barrage of our own negative self-criticism, and get close enough to Him to feel something of the warmth of His love and the reality of His forgiveness. And then we must reject our estimate of ourselves, and take His estimate of us, which—however low it may be concerning our condition—is as high as heaven concerning our possibilities.

The second thing I should want to tell such a person is that the reality of the love of God will not come to us by thinking about it, but only by going among people who believe in it and practise it, and feeling and experiencing it with and through them. The love of God is first realized through the love that other people show us in a disinterested way. We also experience the love of God as we seek to be channels of it ourselves to other people in trouble, sorrow, need, sickness. Such a feeling about God as is expressed in that letter is not an intellectual matter, it is an emotional matter. The person's own negative emotions cause the fear-ridden thoughts of God. This cannot be wiped out by intellectual means primarily, but only by a change of emotion. This can usually be brought about, not so much by effort, but by the fact of some other person's caring. If we think of ourselves as a failure, unattractive, inferior, socially dull, thwarted, nothing will do so much to drive out these thoughts as to have someone else think we are worth working over, worth giving time to, worth helping to find faith and God.

6. Fear will be more and more conquered as we turn our anxiety-thoughts into prayers. We cannot always control the matters that are on our minds: but we can control what we do with those concerns. If we brood on them, talk about them negatively, dwell on them in a self-centered way, they become worse, they increase, they become the fruitful cause of break-down. But if we talk them over at once with God, the negative, faithless, self-centered thoughts will go. A letter tells of someone who uses the hours of pain and wakefulness to pray for others, and how sometimes this results later in healthy sleep. A friend of mine says he used to be the "president, secretary, treasurer and whole board of directors of the 'I'm-very-sorry-for-me Club'." Well, he wasn't the whole membership: I know a lot of members of that club! But he got out of it, because he learned how to pray.

We need to understand prayer as the communion between the Father of our spirits, and ourselves. It is not a lever to pull when we want our own way: it is a relationship which is to be cultivated. Prayer makes possible everything that *is* possible. It brings the maximum health of which you and I, being who and what we are, are capable. It brings the maximum yield in a situation, that situation being just what it is. It helps a person to live and work at the very utmost of his or her capacity. Prayer does not throw the laws and the course of this universe out of kilter because somebody turns on a strong flow of self-will and points it up towards God. Prayer at first often brings relief and comfort. Then prayer is likely to go into a period when there is a good deal of hard work about it. And when a pray-er has stuck it out through the early stages, then prayer, especially for others, is likely to show some remarkable fruits. But people in fear can have the experience of bringing that fear before God, working with Him till slowly they take their hands off it, and get up from their knees with the power of it broken. Fear is recurrent and persistent; and this must be done more than once. But from the very first, we can know that its power is broken. Fear multiplies through the negative interior conversations which we carry on so often with ourselves— an argument which we carry on with someone we dislike— a day-dream of unreality in which we live awhile only to come back to find the actualities more unpleasant than ever—an eloquent discourse to ourselves on our own virtues—or a revelling anticipation of something awful that may happen. When we are alone, or unoccupied, our thoughts ought naturally to turn into prayers—and if they did, we should not have much time left for fear.

More and more one sees that, whatever kind of furnishings the interior life may have, its *climate* is one of faith or of fear. One faces life positively or negatively. One constantly has to push against a doubt whether what we contemplate can succeed, and whether we can carry it through; or one is pulled forward by an extra force of faith which takes delight and derives power from the very game of existence itself. I do not deny that glands have something to do with this, and that there are those whose temperaments are predominantly of one kind or the other. A good, healthy frame strongly disposes up to a positive outlook on life. But this only makes all the greater the victories of faith in the lives of those who are not physically or temperamentally weighted in the direction of positive living. There is literally no type of fear which has not been progressively banished from human consciousness by the right methods. Fear, as Lowes Dickinson said of war, is a problem, not a fate.

So the fearful will do well to let their minds linger long

and often over such a promise as this: "God hath not given us the spirit of fear; but of power, and of love, and of a sound mind."[2] Notice the antithesis between God and fear. Test your own religion by whether it puts God and fear poles and universes apart. God never gives us the spirit of fear—not about this life nor about the life to come. Religion of the wrong kind can increase fear. The kind of religion that is content to listen to the words of the Gospel but lets them roll off without ever resulting in an actually closer working relation with God to relieve the needs of the world—religion that keeps poring over minute sins and so reminding us more and more of our miserable little selves, instead of reminding us of the greatness and love and forgiveness of God—religion that makes us complacent and satisfied and hostile to growth—this kind of religion makes a nest for fear. But God never gave any one that kind of religion.

"But of power. . ." This cannot mean material force which is no antidote to fear. We often think that if only we had larger scope and place, everything would come right: but this rules out worldly position as any cure for fear. This means spiritual power—a power that comes, not by assertion, or position, or ability to command, but by true inner strength, by graciousness, by knowing the rules of the game of life. Often we seek to overcome fear by power, but it is power which we generate: and selfish power can become another source of fear. The only lasting power is power that comes from God. That is the first step away from fear.

"And of love . . ." We find the spirit of love as we begin to care for people, to live for them and in them. The spirit bound in the prison of self and fear must seek to step out into at least one other life and establish real contact. One of the healthiest, happiest men I know is a doctor in his

[2] II Timothy 1:7.

late seventies. He seldom mentions himself. He makes forty or fifty telephone or personal calls a day. His love for God pours over all the time into people. He is one of the most-to-be-envied men I know, and one of the people farthest from fear. Living in others is the second step away from fear.

"And of a sound mind . . ." The Greek word means the self-controlled or disciplined mind, the very opposite of the unsound mind which is that of fear and self-centeredness. Fear disintegrates the mind, adds a fresh fear of losing its control altogether. The power-filled, love-filled mind is the sound mind, the healthy mind. If we have lost this, or see others who have lost it, let us live deeply on this promise that it can be restored. We do not need to stay as we are—that is the great, lasting, superb assurance of a living faith.

We close with a prayer that could do much to change the mind of fear which is so common in our time: "O God, give me the serenity to accept what cannot be changed, the courage to change what can be changed, and the wisdom to know one from the other. Amen."

XI

Helping the Defeated

MOST PEOPLE are defeated in some area. But the fact that they are in the main successful in most of the other areas of their lives enables them to maintain a certain morale. This is a good thing, insofar as pride is a good thing: it is an evil thing, insofar as pride is an evil thing. A defeat which may be covered up from sight or lost in a lot of averagely good qualities may prevent us from ever seeing ourselves as we really are, and from grappling seriously with our faults. But a frank, open defeat which is known to others tears pride down to the ground and lays the trouble bare. Then the need is stark and help is unquestionably necessary.

We are going to talk in this chapter about certain types of need that fall into this class.

Sometimes sorrow and grief are like this. People are so overwhelmed by their loss or tragedy that there is no pretense of control left. The emotional collapse is complete, there is hysterical crying and the person goes to pieces. This often has a physical side to it also. The doctor does what he can: gives them a sedative and puts them to bed. A fresh visitor calls forth the telling of the story again, and a new torrent of tears.

There is a good side to this open emotion. There is a kind of self-control which is not really a victory except on the surface. The grief goes down into the subconscious where it may fester and increase and do much more harm, possibly cause a deferred and much more lengthy and serious collapse. I have sometimes seen a 'dry' grief where it would have been infinitely better if the person could have cried. Tears are often an invaluable safety-valve, and emotions which ought to find a vent find it through them. Often we would do better not to try to make people stop crying: it may relieve them more than anything else of a physical nature.

There is a great difference between a Stoic kind of victory, and a Christian kind of victory. The Stoic (which for us means the tens of thousands of people who try to work by 'will-power') is sometimes a very courageous person: he fights with an iron will, and 'won't let it get him:' he maintains a marble exterior of control which we cannot but admire. But he never quite condescends to *live through* the sorrow, he is constantly pushing it away from him, he wants his control at once; and for such a person sorrow tends to harden him, when it should make him more sympathetic and sensitive. The Christian lives through the whole experience, letting it touch him just as it will; he knows that there is something he needs to learn through this experience and which he will not learn if he pushes the thing from him; his victory does not come from the strength of his own will, but from the grace of God. For the Christian, while he never denies that pain is pain, or sorrow is sadness, he is constantly seeking and finding deeper meanings of the love and grace of God. A Christian does not seek to be impassive and impervious to suffering. He knows that his religion is not insurance against trouble, but only against defeat.

Here is a woman whose son was the apple of her eye. He was needlessly, senselessly killed in the war, by an accident, —killed by a mistake on the part of men in his own regiment. To her loss was added the knowledge that this need not have happened, and could not possibly have done any good. She was inconsolable. Her life, she said, was at an end. Here is real tragedy. We let this pour out with no attempt to stanch it. We could not be cheaply cheerful: her support, her joy in life, were gone in a wasteful accident. All we could do was to look to a Crucifix on the wall and say, "Well, God lost a Son like that. All that was even worse—, the result, not of men's mistakes, but of their wilful evil. God understands just what you are going through." At first it seemed as if nothing got across to her: all her thoughts were upon the boy, how he died, how he must have suffered, what a tragedy it was, what was she going to do? But prayer with her and for her began to reach her heart. The consolation of God began to heal. She began praying herself. The loss was not changed, but the reaction to the loss was changed. When last I saw her, she had found something to live by and something to live for. God had given victory for defeat.

Perhaps the most complete defeat of all is insanity. What can we do for those who have broken down mentally? Sometimes a physical condition has caused it, and the only way to get at it is through physical means—medicine, treatments, an operation if this is indicated. Sometimes it has come about through the abnormal thinking of the person himself, e.g. dwelling upon the desired unreality till the mind takes flight from reality entirely and the person begins living in two worlds, the necessary world of fact, and this other world of day-dreams, and so becomes insane. Sometimes insanity is temporary and can be cured: sometimes it is humanly incurable. Obviously we can only work with the doctor who is responsible for the case.

It is very easy to treat insane people almost as if they were dead. They are put in an institution, which is probably the kindest thing for them and for society. But then how often are they forgotten entirely! Many of them have lucid moments, when some touch with the outside world of reality would be a blessing to them. No matter how distressing the sights about them, no matter how hard it is to leave them pleading to be taken out with us and brought home, we should visit them as often as possible after consultation with the doctor, and give them the feeling that they are cared about by their friends and families.

The institutions for the insane need our help and prayers. About two years ago, a group of praying women felt called upon to pray for the insane, and for the institutions where they are confined. Not long after we began hearing from a group of conscientious objectors who were doing a superb job in one of the mental institutions of the south. They found conditions very bad indeed, improper food and care, not enough help, inadequate people for the staff etc. These conditions were brought to the governor's attention, a thorough investigation was instituted, the offending doctors were removed, a large appropriation was made for improving the hospital, and conditions were greatly bettered. There are going to be more mentally sick people, not less. The institutions where they must live are supported by our taxes: they need also to be supported by our interest and our active concern.

But perhaps our best contribution is towards the prevention of insanity. And this can best be done by helping people to meet the tensions and stresses of life in a strength greater than their own. Many are kept from falling into various degrees of abnormality by a faith that (1) keeps them always facing right into the facts, (2) keeps receiving them from within by the steady victories which faith gives, and (3) keeps them from being self-centered by exercising actual concern for other people. A doctor in a state hospital for the insane told me that ninety per cent of the patients were there because they could not cope with life. Here is where a great faith makes life a different thing altogether : anybody with God can cope with any situation. This prevents escapism and break-down.

Alcoholism is one of the great defeats of the modern world. If we thought Prohibition failed to achieve its end, let us be honest and admit that repeal has done little good. Obviously the problem cannot be met by legislation. The large number of sanitaria that exist primarily to 'cure' alcoholics make a very slight contribution : unless the root of the matter is touched, patients are sobered up and made healthy so that they may go on their next binge. There are rescue missions that can instance men who have been converted from drink and stayed converted for the rest of their lives : I know such men intimately and personally. Yet neither does this touch the wide-spread problem of alcoholism upon a sufficient scale to make any real contribution to its solution.

The greatest contribution, in my opinion, that is being made in our time is that of the group called Alcoholics Anonymous. Somewhere near twenty thousand men and women in this country have been "dried up" by this amazing piece of work. It grew in part out of the ashes of some very inadequate work for alcoholics which some of us were trying to do about fifteen years ago : one of them made up his mind to collect all the scientific data on the subject that could be collected. This was written down, with cases to illustrate, in the book *Alcoholics Anonymous,* which is the guide-book for all beginners. In dozens of cities you will now find pleasant club houses where on certain nights in the week there are meetings where alcoholics are welcome, and certain 'open meetings' where all are welcome. Three or four men or women will talk simply, unemotionally, convincingly about their own experience, pointing out the actual steps that must be taken if one wants to be cured. They look upon alcoholism as a disease. These individual men and women will give any amount of time to going to see other alcoholics who want help—they will not waste a moment of time on those who are "not drunkards, of course—I can handle this myself—just slipped off this once;" nor will they try to persuade anyone that he is an alcoholic. But once he admits the fact, there is no trouble to which they will not go to help him find the answer. Essential in the cure is the trust in a Higher Power, by whatever name they call it: this comes into the speeches and literature in such a way as not to prejudice those who have difficulty with religious terms: the end result is usually to help a man find the reality of the faith in which he was brought up. They say that about seventy-five per cent of those who really give it an honest try are 'dried up.' It is folly for an inexperienced person, of whatever good will or kind sentiment, to try by himself to 'cure drunks' when this group knows the ropes and can do it ever so much better. We can all supplement the work of "A.A.", but we should be foolish to attempt to duplicate it.

I have sometimes wondered at the finality with which the "A.A.'s" assume that alcoholism is a disease, especially when I see how little trust they put in medical or material remedies, and how almost wholly it is a matter of what the alcoholic does for himself, with the assistance of others who have been in his case and with the help of the 'Higher Power.' But I had a vivid reminder of the reality of the disease one Sunday morning. With an ex-alcoholic friend of mine, I had gone to the early celebration of Holy Communion. This man is well changed, and so mature both psychologically and spiritually that he is helping other people in rather a large way. When he received the Holy Communion, he took a very small sip of wine. After the service he was trembling like a leaf, and said to me, "If I didn't have something—Somebody—to grab on to right now, I'd go and take a drink." I advised him thereafter to receive the Communion only in one kind, and not to touch the wine. But I also saw how deeply ingrained the taste for alcohol was in his body. I think this should be remembered by any who seek to help alcoholics.

There is such a thing as defeat in relationships. Divorce, quarrels, litigation between friends or members of a family, are indications of it. When a man and his wife cannot get on, they sometimes can keep it from the eye of the public, but certainly not from their children or their intimate friends. Thousands of homes know what hell on earth is because somebody has an ungovernable temper. If there is another person who makes us bristle with irritation, that relationship constitutes for us a defeat—not a misfortune, or a mere 'clash of temperaments,' but a real defeat. We may pray about it, and make high resolves; but let the person come within fifty feet, and our hackles go up, and there are 'words.'

The world has its solution for these things. It says that such people should simply keep away from each other. It says that such relationships in the past should be buried and forgotten. It says that, where things are not intolerable, the best thing is to humor the husband or wife with a constitutional temper, avoid the situations and subjects which call it forth, and make the best of it : but if no other solution offers, get a divorce. All this is just one way of accepting the defeat.

The Christian solution is conversion. It is the cure of temper by getting at the fear, self-love, domination, self-will, that cause it. There is literally no sin in the calendar to which an answer has not been found in Christian conversion. There does not have to be conversion at first on both sides : it can start with one. If the relationship is put in God's hands, and our own emotional reactions to it surrendered, He can begin to work. There will probably be an apology for the places where we have been wrong—no matter whether the other person has been still more wrong. I made an apology like that once myself, and all I got in reply was, "I am glad you have come to your senses: I have been telling you this for years." No matter: the apology *freed me* from resentment and bitterness. And this opens the channel for God to work. Most people will respond to an acknowledgment of wrong by admitting where they were wrong, also. In such an atmosphere the points of disagreement can frankly be brought into the open, discussed, settled and laid.

Defeat in relationships is of the same quality as the vast defeat called war. Some years ago I heard a businessman who worked in a shipping office give a vivid illustration of the way personal relationships affect even international relations. At the breakfast table in New Jersey, he lost his temper with his wife. At the office he turned the heat on his executive force. They put the heat in a cable to a ship-captain whose ship lay in the harbor of Yokahama. He passed it on to his men, and within a few hours of the time when the family had a row in New Jersey, a lot of angry sailors were on shore in Japan. To say the least of it, sailors like that are not the best ambassadors of international peace.

Sex is another field where we can be defeated. It constitutes one of the most difficult things to handle, because sex is natural, it is inherent in every human body. Alcohol and drugs are imported from without: sex is as inseparable from us as our hearts or livers. And at its best, sex is not only the means by which the race is continued, but it is the natural expression of deep love, and a great source of creative inspiration. The right kind of sex has nothing wrong in it, and is one of the most wonderful experiences in the world.

But sex is essentially a means, not an end. It is a means of creating children, it is a means of binding two people who love each other more closely together, it is a means of releasing the emotions to their highest creative capacity. Because sex is pleasurable, it easily becomes an end in itself. And where sex becomes an end in itself, an emotion which is generated because of its own pleasurableness, rather than one which is incidental to a great love and a relationship which has in it many other non-physical qualities, it goes wrong. The indulgence of sex for its own sake constitutes a defeat—and a very common one.

What can be offered to people as a curb and off-set to this most powerful and persistent of all urges? No counsels of fear, and scarcely any appeals for character, can do it. Only something that can make just as great an appeal to the individual as sex can. Studdert Kennedy used to say that "it takes a passion to conquer a passion." I should imagine that intense concentration upon a scientific problem would absorb all a man's energies completely. But then, when the solution is found, what does he do? I have known a clean love-affair to clear up a terrible sex-defeat; and when the sex element in the love-relation was right, the whole thing was on so different a level that it was not like the old license at all. But if there is one emotion that is as strong as sex, and can hold people from it where it is wrong, it is the love of God. We can come to love God more than we love anything else in this world; and loving Him means wanting to do His will and build His Kingdom. If this asks of us discipline, continence, in the area of sex, we are able to meet the demand because of two things (1) the greatness of the end in view—the Kingdom is bigger than our personal desires, and (2) the greatness of the help given—the grace of God is a very different thing from human 'will-power.' This does not mean repression nor self-effort: this means resting on God for full joy in life, and expecting Him to satisfy all our deepest and realest needs.

Helping the Defeated

The problem of drugs is one with a sad history. Not long ago a trained nurse was found dead in her room. I knew that woman and the struggle she had made. Years ago in a hospital when she was sick, she was given drugs to help her. The drugs became a habit. She would sell her soul for them while the craving was on her: and the moment there was the least let-up, she would renounce them with everything there was in her. In the end the drugs won, and they killed her. Sometimes she looked to God for help. Where lay the failure? It lay somewhere in the fitfulness with which she sought God and the fellowship of His people. We would not hear from her for months, even years: then when she got in trouble, she would come back. We did what we could; but if she had built up her faith during the times between, made strong friends with Christian people and kept her associations with them, the outcome might have been different.

Others have found that spiritual faith was sufficient for them to throw off even the binding curse of drugs. I know another woman who had as powerful a craving as one could imagine; but she made up her mind she was going to whip it. And with all the help she could find in prayer, and all the force and determination she could muster (she was naturally a strong character), she won. Not long before his death, I talked often with Captain Richmond Pierson Hobson, whose name we associate with the Spanish American war. The last years of his life were largely devoted to the problem of narcotics. He told me that the number of cures affected apart from religious faith was negligible.

The strength of the curse of drugs should be a reminder to those who let themselves become dependent upon such things as sleeping pills. There are times of special strain, when on a doctor's advice, some aids to sleep are aids to recovery and health. Strict care should be taken to get the non-habit-forming variety. The habit-forming drug is continually laying hold of people and dragging them down. The last person I talked to who had this problem was a brilliant and gifted professional man who, finding himself thwarted in carrying out a special type of work, took to drink and then to drugs. Real faith is giving him a raft on which he can climb out; but we got him just in time.

Another common defeat is depression. In such a mood, life seems unbearable, intolerable. Nothing, nobody, seems to matter. The pain is sometimes worse than a physical pain. Suicide offers a way out, but not really because it takes effort—more effort than to remain in a 'brown study' of depressing thoughts and negative day-dreams. There may be physical reasons for this: a low blood-pressure inclines us towards it, or a very low metabolism, or over-fatigue. Doctors may find part of the cause of depression, and the modern "shock-treatment" may greatly relieve it. But there are other factors which no medicine can touch. I knew a man subject to terrific fits of depression: they were traceable to two things (1) vast over-eating, so that his body was taxed beyond its capacity and became sluggish, and (2) inexcusable idleness which prevented him from applying himself to any long-range task, preferring to live without purpose on his modest income. A subtler cause of depression, but very common, is the poor handling of strongly aggressive instincts. For instance, a man who has applied himself with unlimited concentration to his work, over-doing it, meticulous and highly conscientious, with no time for play and little for his family and children, will begin finding himself unable to apply himself, he feels fatigue, he feels badly, he says he is sick. The psychological truth is, he has worn his work thread-bare, seeking to make it his whole 'sublimation' of his aggressiveness, drawn the one string on which he plays tighter and tighter until it has snapped. Often he will charge this up to others—the

family, the people for whom he works, the general unap-
preciativeness of the world—but the real explanation is
that he needs other social, aesthetic, human, intellectual,
recreational, religious, outlets to use up his instinctual energies. The most difficult thing will be to get him to see
that he is himself the cause of his depression, and that what
he thinks of as his noble conscientiousness is really a very
thin veneer for his egotism. Religion and psychiatry are
at one in this: they see behind the defenses and pretenses
of 'high motives,' rationalizations in self-defense, excuses.
The psychologically mal-adjusted and blind, and the
spiritual Pharisee and hypocrite, are exactly alike in their
determination to defend, excuse, and accept themselves as
they are. The psychologically mature and adjusted, and
the spiritually sincere and converted, are exactly alike in
their willingness to admit that they may be wrong, in their
desire to find out about themselves and face themselves, and
in their readiness to face cheerfully the difficulty of radical
change and improvement.

If we were honest about it, many of us would admit that
our worst defeat is living in a rut, content to be no more
than what we have been and are. A young man tells me of
working in a business office. He is twenty-seven, has a
pleasant personality and above average ability. He drifted
into this job, and cannot quite make up his mind to leave
it for something better. He doesn't quite know what he
thinks "something better" would be. I advised him to
consider two things: (1) what is the thing he can do best?
and (2) what is the best thing he can do? At this moment
I am trying to put some more stiffening into his will. For
to stay where he is constitutes, I am sure, a genuine defeat.
He can waste his life on something that does not seem
worth spending time on, really because he has not the
courage to stir his stumps, look over the whole field, and
choose a job that seems worth doing.

Sometimes the change-over comes, not from taking a different job, but through spiritual vision gaining a new conception of the possibilities of the job you hold. A man found himself in possession of a hotel that was off the beaten track and running down. He had begun to believe in prayer. One day he told God he would "make a bargain with Him: if He would carry me through this, I'd give Him the proceeds." The hotel flourishes, is filled for the season more than a year ahead. He says, "No disappointment remains with me for more than the first shock. I have turned everything over to God, and it works out."

The thing which I want most to say about defeat is that we must never let defeat spin its own philosophy. Defeat always creates a belief small enough to fit its own case. Possibly the most tragic human being I ever saw was a psycho-pathic boy of good family who has become so completely institutionalized that he is terrified of the outside world. Through careless treatment, he is sometimes considered better and let loose into society again. He then writes someone he knows threatening to commit a crime, in order that he may be picked up by the police, in order that they may look up his record, and again commit him to an institution where he will feel safe. I have sought to give him some spiritual help, with little success. When the police were talking with him the last time he was picked up, one of them said to him, "Do you ever pray, or go to Church?"·He said that he did not. "Why?" said the detective. "Because I do not believe in God." Poor lad—of course he didn't believe in God. He literally *couldn't* believe in God. Nobody living in the depths of mental and moral defeat where he lives could possibly believe in God. What you believe colors the way you live, but the way you live colors what you believe, too! This is an exaggerated case, but it shows vividly how a low level of life causes a low level of faith.

Helping the Defeated

What is needed by all people in defeat, and all of us are defeated in some way, is not a belief commensurate with our defeat, but a belief so big that it lifts us above our defeat. A valuable but very heavy safe was lost from a boat in a harbor, and stuck fast in the mud. The grappling irons and derrick could not dislodge and raise it. But irons were got about it and the chains were attached, at low tide, to a strong raft. When the tide came in, the safe swung loose from the mud and was salvaged from the water. So the little grappling-hooks of inadequate personal philosophy are not strong enough to lift us above our defeats. We need the irons of God wrapped about us, and the tides of God to sweep in and dislodge us. We must leave our old defeats stuck in the mud—leave them long enough to go and search out the greater irons and the stronger chains and to wait for the tide. When we have done what we can, the tide about which we can do nothing, must do the rest. It will lift us from the floor of our defeat. Only God can lift us out of our defeats. He can—and if we let Him—He will.

XII

Helping the Conscientious and Self-Deceived

A WISE MAN once said that it is easier to help bad people than good people. The reason is obvious. Bad people find themselves in collision, not only with the *mores* of society, but with their own consciences and the laws of God: when they do wrong, they know that they are doing wrong. Whatever excuses he makes for himself, an alcoholic cannot be deceived about the reality of his problem. All his relations with the outside world remind him of it. But a good person—that is, a person with a fairly clear conscience, with what is on the whole a good reputation, who stands well in the eyes of 'the world'—is inclined to look upon every fault as a slight lapse from uniform good behaviour. Under these circumstances, one may dispense help, but one does not stand in need of it. One is doing pretty well. And if this is not said to us often enough, we say it to ourselves.

It is by this swift descent that good people become Pharisees. The Pharisees were not the monsters of sham and deception that we often think of them as being. They were good people who knew that they were good—that is all. Jewry had no better spiritual aristocrats than the Pharisees. They really *were* the best people—only they knew it. This Pharisaism is a category to which none of us thinks he belongs. Some are not so averse to being prodigals—indeed a prodigal past is often looked upon rather as an asset. But we do not want to be Pharisees! Therefore we say we are not. We try to persuade most of the rest of mankind to side with us, for they too do not want to be looked upon as Pharisees; and a little conspiracy against being considered hypocrites is quite a pleasant company. Probably no one in the world was more surprised to be called 'hypocrites' than the original Pharisees, the people who unwittingly gave their names to this whole prideful and scandalous business of thinking how good one is. They kept the Commandments and they did their spiritual duty, and the rest of the Jews were not so strict nor so dutiful— all this was sober fact. Yet Jesus thundered at them. They were the only people He ever thundered at. He never thundered at harlots and sinners generally. He some-times told them to stop what they were doing, but you never feel any personal heat in it. Yet when He turns on the Pharisees, you feel the whole force of a morally out-raged personality is being flung after an objective judg-ment. There was something about Pharisaic hypocrisy that stank to high heaven. It still does.

Let us remember, when we plan to help the conscientious and self-deceived, that we begin in the unenviable and thankless position of wanting to help where help is not only unwanted, but would be most firmly declined if it were offered. Talk about patience!—nobody in the world re-quires the patience which these people require. To sit and listen to the fine-spun self-justification of one of these people who attributes everything he does to a fine motive takes more self-control than any other exercise in which I— at least—have ever engaged. Real sinners are often so lovable: and these dear old hypocrites, how extremely un-lovable, how sometimes really exasperating, they are! Yet this must not creep into our thoughts or emotions about them as we talk to them, and it must not come out in our words to them or about them. We cut something by thinking or speaking in this way.

Here is a man who has worked in the same office for thirty years. He gets up at an unnecessarily early hour and is there before anyone else; he leaves at an absurdly late hour in the evening and often takes a lot of work home with him. He will tell you with a perfectly straight face that he thinks this extra work is incumbent upon him, and he will smile with satisfaction when somebody uses the word 'sacrifice' in connection with his long hours. He has not now the money he once had to indulge in handsome presents to his friends, but he still spends more than he should on gifts. The adulation of his friends gives him mighty pleasure, and the more times the word 'generosity' is used of him, naturally the happier he is. The real fact is that the overtime represents an escape from an emotionally empty life: it is as much a form of escapism as an addict's dram of heroin. And the real fact is that the gifts represent a very great pride in a past when his family was wealthy and could give lavishly. The things he tells himself (and others) about his sacrifices for the company, and about how much his friends enjoy his attentions are, of course, much pleasanter to believe than the real facts. It was an enormous shock to him when I once suggested these things to him. I had to choose between leaving him a quite false and flimsy security, and running the risk of demolishing all the security he had. It almost made him sick. But he began to face it. He smarts a little under it yet: but I think a mental operation like this was the one thing that could open his eyes to what he was doing to himself. He was working too much for the good of his health, and he was living too much on the adulation of other people for the good of his soul.

Here is a woman who has contributed a considerable public service. The people in a whole state have cause to be thankful for what she has done in a public way. She always felt she was not sufficiently appreciated at home, where

the sharpness of her temper and the irritability of her character did not contribute to receiving the flattery on which
she lived. So she sought what she craved—attention,
praise, gratitude—in public service. When some of her
family mildly suggested that if perhaps she gave a little
of this concern to the rest of the family, it might contribute to harmony and happiness, there was only a grunt
that she "never was appreciated by the family." There
was a complete divorce between what happened in her office, and what happened when she crossed her own threshold. Naturally her estimate of herself was that of a noble
servant of her special causes and her state. But the real truth
was that she grew up with a feeling of inferiority which
could be assuaged in only one way, e.g. by buckets of flattery. Normal encouragement at home was not enough.
Everyone must be interested in her interests, everyone must
accept her word, everyone must think she was perfect.
Nobody likes a dictator at home, any better than they like
one across the seas. The truth is, she is a capable, sensitive,
intensely proud person, getting even with a rather bad inferiority complex. She knows a good deal of psychology
when it comes to getting things done, but there is a great
gap in her psychology when applied to herself. If there is
one thing on which the whole gravamen of the Christian
religion, and the deepest insights of modern psychology,
unite in perfect agreement it is in the one assumption which
both would like to urge upon the whole human race,
namely this, "You may be wrong: and you are most likely
to be wrong at the point where you are most sure you are
right."

Let us remind ourselves of some of the forms of conscientious self-deception:

1. The rationalization of our personal desires into matters of principle. I once knew a worrying, honourable, capable, half-sick woman who loved to plan for her children's

lives to the last harrowing detail. She nearly drove them crazy; but she could always attach her personal wish to something no less lofty than one of the Ten Commandments. The least knowledge of herself would have shown her that the whole thing was an elaborate projection of self-will, thwarted by her physical weakness.

2. Not seeing in ourselves what we do not wish others to see. I have a delightful clerical friend with whom I was talking as we both came from a surprisingly genuine meeting with some other clerical friends. We had 'let down our hair' to a remarkable degree; and this one brother was not sure he wanted to have his companions "know all about my weaknesses." I smiled at him and said, "You couldn't hide them if you tried. Everybody on earth that knows you knows you want good food and good parishes." Self-indulgence and personal ambition to be a worldly success are very easy qualities to read.

3. Work as the projection of the power-motive. There is a woman who loves to pour herself out for other people, by understanding them and helping them to understand themselves. Many of these people find her helpful up to a point—and then they begin to recoil and slip away. I think there is in her make-up a powerful streak of domination which is bound to come out sooner or later, because it has never been faced nor given up. What she thinks of as purely unselfish service is in part the outworking of her unfaced craving for power.

4. Concern for the under-dog which takes itself out in arm's-length charity, but forgets problems nearer home. I knew a man who believed himself to be the most complete "democrat:" he always sought out people who were on a lower social plane than himself, he said that such people were finer and had more gentle feelings than the socially privileged. Yet the truth was that he had a whacking big inferiority complex which caused him to feel uncomfortable

with his own kind, but comfortable among those to whom he could easily be superior. To show how little he cared really for simple folk, I once heard him refer to the men who worked in his own store as "that kind of cattle." One would like to have quoted to him Emerson's lines: "If an angry bigot assumes this bountiful cause of Abolition, and comes to me with his last news from Barbadoes, why should not I say this to him. 'Go love thy infant; love thy wood chopper; be good-natured and modest; have that grace; and never varnish your hard, uncharitable ambition with this incredible tenderness for black folk a thousand miles off. Thy love afar is spite at home' "![1]

5. The pride of feeling humble. To be disgusted with oneself, to feel like a failure, to dislike oneself, is sin, not virtue. Most people do not know what humility is: for it only arises in the Presence of God. What passes for humility is usually the self-disgust that comes from wounded pride or thwarted self-will. To know that one is often or usually disgusted with oneself may only indicate a vast ambition unrealized. To be satisfied with one's humility is only to be satisfied with oneself, which is pure pride.

6. Blaming fortune for our faults. A man told me he was having trouble with his wife, adding, "But she was born under Leo, and Leos like to dominate." I just said, "Would you please tell her with my compliments that a lot of us who were not born under Leo still love to dominate—the Leos have no copyright on domination—dominators have been born under every sign in the Zodiac. She'll get farther if she calls it wilfulness, and remembers Mr. Shakespeare's observation that the fault lies not in our stars but in ourselves."

7. Crowding out large duties by small. People have missed the end of great speeches because they 'always let the dog out at 9:30.' They have missed great spiritual op-

[1] Essay on Self-Reliance.

portunities by an ingrown habit of staying at home. They have spent hours with sick people or children, forgetful that an hour away seeing something fresh and new would enrich their vigil. Never forget that the Woman at the Well "left her water-pot" when she met Jesus: He gave her a much bigger job to do for a while!

But how to help these people?

One thing we must do: we must recognize their good points, which really are good points, and encourage them about the contributions which they make. The generality of people flatters the conscientious and self-deceived, and this flattery helps them to keep up the self-deception—"after all, if all these people say I am so fine, I must *be* fine." We must risk some of this in order to be just; and it is peculiarly necessary to be just with such people, else when we raise any questions with them, they will take it for some kind of personal prejudice or attack. The only way to stop a run-away horse is to run with him: if we ever hope to gain a place of confidence from which we can open up on difficult subjects, we can only do it by genuine appreciation of all that they do and all that is best in them. Running with people should if possible include working with them somewhere, because it is in actual human situations that human faults come out; and situations caused by the unconscious faults of the self-deceived may be our avenue of approach to their unrecognized problems.

We need also a quiet but firm resistance to the symptoms of the deeper need. We shall deal with the deeper need later: just now we are seeking ways to reveal the person to himself. Let me give an illustration. A competent and creative woman, who does a good job looking after her family, and has wide community interests, has a sharp tongue, talks critically of most people and gossips a good deal. This kind of talk is but a symptom of a self-deceived person, who has never faced herself. She expects and she tends to draw other people along with her in these 'panning parties' of hers. One of her friends simply stands up to her, and when this kind of thing begins, says simply, "I don't think we ought to talk about people like this, and I am not going to do it." There is a simple moral courage that can stop a good deal of mischief. We do not always need to talk like Olympians : sometimes a humorous rejoinder will go farther than a serious one. I had a visiting clergyman once who had no degree : seeing an unused bachelor's hood in the vestry-room he asked if he might wear it. I winked at him and just said, "Maybe you haven't got any conscience, but I have." We need to be alert, and not to give away our position by small compromises like falling in with less serious phases of the very thing we want to cure. This must not turn into *nagging,* waiting for a chance to 'say something,' hitting at things in a hinting and roundabout way. This will kill our chances of ever doing anything radical and constructive.

Somewhere we have got to jolt the conscientious and self-deceived. I am afraid there is no other way to put it. I wish the easier, more indirect ways would work : but self-deception is always at least aware enough to protect itself ; and will ignore hints and suggestions oftentimes. An old drunkard came asking me to help his drunken son ; he had a theory that he could 'hold it' and his son couldn't. I had worked on this young man for some time, and then discovered that the father continued to keep liquor on the sideboard and to take it himself in the presence of his son whenever he chose. I said to that man just what you are thinking.

A lordly matron whose husband gave a fair amount of time helping us in our work called me on the phone one day to say that I was "killing her husband," and that I was a fanatic. She was a wealthy woman who gave generously but most unwisely of her money, and lived on the adulation of her beneficiaries. It happened that I had helped her and people she was interested in a good many times. It did not cross her mind that a clergyman would not be amenable to her domination, as her servants and many of her friends were. I had to write her a letter she told me she would never forget, the gist of which was that she had been spoiled by her parents, her husband and her fawning friends all her life, and never heard the unvarnished truth about herself; which I proceeded to tell her. Nothing softer was of any avail: I had tried everything else before I took this course.

For five years I sought to bring spiritual vitality into the life of a church-going woman, of impeccable social background and very good heart, but soft and without spiritual power. She and her husband, my wife and I, became good friends socially; we liked the same things, we enjoyed each other. Vainly I sought a challenge that would puncture the conventionality and complacency of this woman. Then her husband died. This need brought her to me, after she had tried the world's way of trying to forget and to enjoy herself. I prayed a lot about it; and it seemed right to deal in the truth. As we sat there talking, I said, "You know, you are the kind of woman that is the matter with America and the matter with the Church." She asked what I meant, and I said, "You're more concerned about your clothes and your cocktail and the beauty of your apartment than you are about Christ and His Kingdom." She said she'd never been talked to in this way in her life, and flounced out in great anger. But next day she was back, told me she knew what I said was true, and hurt so because of its truth. She made her genuine decision for Christ that day, and life has been a different thing ever since. I hate to use the knife like this: it takes more out of me than anything else that I have to do in connection with people. But at times only a real operation will cure.

Helping the Conscientious and Self-Deceived

One of the things that reveals the conscientious and self-deceived to themselves is to come into a fellowship of people who are on to themselves, i.e., who just know they are sinners. We were having a week-end for business men in a southern hotel. One man came who knew all the language of religion, and could 'talk pious' with ease. But conceit stood out all over him. He talked—he even walked —for effect. His words had a precision and a pernickety quality that irritated everyone. Soon he found he was in an atmosphere where all this simply 'didn't go.' He began telling us of his long 'stand' for religion, and how his brothers detested him for it, and were always trying to knock him 'off the wagon,' and how one of them recently had succeeded. He was deeply chagrined at this. He began to see that he was more hurt in his pride at breaking his own previous record, than he was for letting Christ down by what he did. He began to see that his Pharisaism was what made his brothers hate his religion. He became conscious of being a fellow-sinner with the rest of us, as simple and lovable a fellow as you could imagine. He wrote his brothers apologizing for his Pharisaism and asking their forgiveness. He is a different man altogether from the fastidious person who came to the conference.

I was told that on the top of the Christian Association building in one city there was to be an absolutely silent prayer-room, with one picture in it: a picture of the Pharisee and the Publican. Said the founder and planner of the building to me, "We want them to come in to that room Pharisees, and go out Publicans." That is just exactly what had happened to this man—he came in a Pharisee, and went out a Publican. "God be merciful to me, a sinner."

I cannot say how important it is—and how hard—to keep personal feelings, like anger and scorn, out of our dealings with people of this kind. Sometimes I have failed to do it, and whenever I have, there have been negative re-

sults. Simple, firm, courageous statement of fact is a step
in God's redemption of them: "the truth shall make you
free." But personal judgment, animus, accusation really
have no place. It is our job to help people see themselves,
and if they will not draw the inferences, we may have to
draw the inferences for them: but the truth needs only to be
spoken, not to be fought over.

Yet at the same time one must emphasize the importance of having courage to grip difficult situations and
to deal with them. It is far easier to let matters drift, to wait
for a 'more convenient season.' We know that half the
heart-aches in the world could be stopped if people would
say what they think to the person whom it involves, instead of saying it to other people. The diagnosis of a self-
deceived person is not hard for other people—for almost all
other people. They see the truth, and will alternately tear
the person to pieces, and laugh about the situation, together. But how many of them will stand against the gossip session, and then have the courage to go to the person
and say lovingly, honestly the truth? How many of them,
asked by the person whether they concur in this expressed
opinion, will stand by the truth, and how many, to keep
favour, will welch and trim and say they could not think
such a harsh thing? How often have I seen men and
women, genuinely convicted or partially convicted of real
faults in their lives, go to their clergyman and ask whether
he thinks this thing which someone told them is true—and
he, also, has flinched from standing by the truth, because
he feared to lose their friendship and support! I don't know
what the 'sin against the Holy Spirit' is, but the place where
it always seems to me men most sin against Him is in letting down the work He has begun by pooh-poohing true
spiritual conviction of sin which the Holy Spirit has initiated. I say it without hesitation, this kind of courage is as
great as that required in war, and much rarer. The blunt

statement of what we think, in resentment, anger or personal pique, requires nothing more than the loss of self-control: but to say the truth lovingly and redemptively when we know it hurts or is unwelcome, or to stand by it where others have first spoken it, requires immense courage.

It takes a considerable maturity to carry this out—a great understanding of life and people, a great self-control, a great fairness of judgment, and a considerable power to speak in measured, adequate words. There is not only the need to wait until we have sufficient diagnosis and enough facts to plunge in: there is also the need to remember the element of *timing*—for the right thing said at the wrong time or in the wrong way is not far from being the wrong thing. Good people, if they are self-deceived, are likely to be peculiarly sensitive to criticism, and to resent it much more than others; so that it is needful to be very sure of our ground, and very sure of the rightness of our own spirit through long, adequate prayer, before we make any attempt to help them.

It almost appears as if, thus far, we have equated the conscientious and the self-deceived. The question may be asked: Are there no sincerely conscientious people? Yes, there are; and sometimes they need help, too. I met one of them recently—a fine young woman with a good mind and a frail body, who met life in the spirit of a thorough-bred race horse. She worked long hours, she took too little time off, she bothered about the problems of the office when she should have been playing and sleeping, and was wearing out her health. She had a keen love for Christ and for people, and she was a real Christian in her ideals and in most of her life. But she was too much driven by self-effort, she was dissatisfied with her life because she felt she had once had a real spiritual experience but had somewhere lost it in a morass of conscientious activity. I began talking to

How You Can Help Other People

her about the three levels of life: the level of instinct, the
level of conscience, and the level of grace; and said that I
believed Christ is as eager to get us up from the level of
conscience to the level of grace, as He is to get us up from
the level of instinct to the level of grace. This opened a new
chapter for her: she said she had never known there were
but two levels: good and bad, and she was trying to be
good. We pointed out that there were two levels of 'goodness,' the conscientious goodness of self-effort, and the
grace-ful goodness that comes from depending completely
on God. One could almost see a load slip from those slender
shoulders of hers which were so eager to "bear the burdens
of others." She is becoming free now to do it.

Other things being equal, it is a harder thing to pull a
good person up from the level of conscience to the level of
grace than it is to pull a bad person up from the level of instinct to the level of grace, especially where complacency
has settled in. We shall meet with more misunderstanding,
more hot opposition, more discouragement and disillusionment about people, in seeking to put the truth before
people like this than before any others. But such people
sometimes do greater harm than pagans or out-and-out
sinners. If we want to see the world re-made, we cannot ignore people like this. And often these people are themselves
dimly aware that something is really wrong at bottom.
Someone said that it is the business of religion to comfort
the afflicted, and to afflict the comfortable. Nothing but
the superhuman and supernatural level of the Christian religion once glimpsed can give these people any idea of
how far short they fall of attaining even their own ideals.
Part of the daily tribute which every ordinary Christian
pays to a religion infinitely above and beyond him lies in
his genuine dissatisfaction with himself before God. When
this is lacking, he has really never begun. For a man to
feel any degree of self-satisfaction in what he has done

[188]

about so mighty a challenge and so profound a help as Christianity is to reveal himself for an unawakened child. All this is what lay behind the poignant and pathetic conversation of Jesus with the Pharisees at the end of the ninth chapter of St. John:

"And Jesus said, For judgment I am come into this world, that they which see not might see; and that they which see might be made blind. And some of the Pharisees which were with him heard these words, and said unto him, Are we blind also? Jesus said unto them, If ye were blind, ye should have no sin: but now ye say, We see; therefore your sin remaineth."